Strength-Based Pedagogy for Smart Students with Disabilities

Using the approach to teaching and developing strengths and talents known as the Schoolwide Enrichment Model (SEM), this book provides a blueprint on how to expand your repertoire of evidence-based practices and pedagogical strategies to better challenge and engage twice-exceptional students.

Covering topics such as how to provide various types of enrichment for the classroom, how to assess individual interests, how to use strength-based learning to promote socioemotional wellbeing, postsecondary transition, and more, this book offers practical advice, easily implemented strategies, and real-life examples from evidence-based research to support educators in helping their students achieve both academic and personal success.

Featuring various methods for providing various types of enrichment in the classroom as well as reproducible materials for immediate implementation, *Strength-Based Pedagogy for Smart Students with Disabilities* offers comprehensive assistance and support to educators and parents in their efforts to guide students and children toward academic and personal success.

Sally M. Reis, Ph.D. holds the Letitia N. Morgan Chair in Educational Psychology, is a Board of Trustees Distinguished Professor, and is well known for her work with academically talented students. She is a past president of the National Association for Gifted Children (NAGC), and the Co-Director of Confratute, the longest running summer institute in the development of gifts and talents.

Susan Baum, Ph.D. is an educator, author, consultant, Chancellor of Bridges Graduate School for Cognitive Diversity in Education and director of the 2e Center for Research and Professional

Development. The author of *To Be Gifted and Learning Disabled*, her globally recognized writing and research covers many areas of education, including differentiated curriculum and instruction, gifted education, gifted learning-disabled students, and gifted underachieving students. Her work on twice-exceptional students is recognized globally and she has received many awards for her contributions to the field of twice exceptionality and strength-based, talent-focused teaching and learning.

Joseph Madaus, Ph.D. is a tenured professor and the director of the Collaborative on Postsecondary Education and Disability in the Neag School of Education at UConn. He has been recognized for his service to the field of higher education and disability and for his research.

Nicholas Gelbar, Ph.D. is a psychologist and researcher at the Neag School of Education at the University of Connecticut. He worked for over five years at the Autism Center at the Hospital for Special Care as a psychologist and is a nationally certified school psychologist as well as a board certified behavior analyst at the Doctoral Level. He has training and expertise in identifying and teaching students identified as neurodiverse and twice-exceptional.

Strength-Based Pedagogy for Smart Students with Disabilities

Using Interest-based Strategies for Academic and Personal Success

Sally M. Reis, Susan Baum, Joseph Madaus, and Nicholas Gelbar

Designed cover image: Getty

First published 2025
by Routledge
605 Third Avenue, New York, NY 10158

and by Routledge
4 Park Square, Milton Park, Abingdon, Oxon, OX14 4RN

Routledge is an imprint of the Taylor & Francis Group, an informa business

© 2025 Sally M. Reis, Susan Baum, Joseph Madaus, and Nicholas Gelbar

The right of Sally M. Reis, Susan Baum, Joseph Madaus, and Nicholas Gelbarto be identified as authors of this work has been asserted in accordance with sections 77 and 78 of the Copyright, Designs and Patents Act 1988.

All rights reserved. No part of this book may be reprinted or reproduced or utilised in any form or by any electronic, mechanical, or other means, now known or hereafter invented, including photocopying and recording, or in any information storage or retrieval system, without permission in writing from the publishers.

Trademark notice: Product or corporate names may be trademarks or registered trademarks, and are used only for identification and explanation without intent to infringe.

Library of Congress Cataloging-in-Publication Data
A catalog record for this book has been requested

ISBN: 978-1-032-84243-1 (hbk)
ISBN: 978-1-032-84244-8 (pbk)
ISBN: 978-1-003-51186-1 (ebk)

DOI: 10.4324/9781003511861

Typeset in Palatino
by Apex CoVantage, LLC

We dedicate this book to our families with thanks for their love and support.

Contents

List of Figures, Tables, and Appendices viii
List of Contributors xi
Acknowledgments xiii
Introduction xiv

1 Using Strength-Based Pedagogy for Students with Disabilities: An Introduction and Overview of Strategies 1

2 Using Strength-Based Learning to Promote Socioemotional Well-being and Success: Challenges Faced and Strategies That Work 37

3 Identifying Students' Strengths and Interests: Getting Started 66

4 Planning Enrichment Experiences That Work for All Students 82

5 Implementing Project-Based Learning and Type III Enrichment in Your Classroom 108

6 All About College 135

7 Concluding Thoughts 163

   Appendices 173

Figures, Tables, and Appendices

Figures

Figure	Title	Origination of figure
1.1	Combination of Exceptionalities (Schader and Baum, 2015)	Original
1.2	Engaging Students through Strengths (Baum and Schader, 2023)	Original
1.3	Leveraging Strengths (Baum and Schader, 2023)	Original
1.4	Dual Differentiation (Baum and Schader, 2023)	Original
1.5	Enrichment and Talent Development Opportunities (Baum and Schader, 2023)	Original
2.1	Phase 1: Forethought/Pre-Action	Original
2.2	Phase 2: Performance Control	Original
3.1	Learning about your Special Interests and Abilities: A Sample Classroom Discussion Part 1	Original
3.2	Learning about your Special Interests and Abilities: A Sample Classroom Discussion Part 2	Original
3.3	Learning about your Special Interests and Abilities: A Sample Classroom Discussion Part 3	Original
3.4	Learning about your Special Interests and Abilities: A Sample Classroom Discussion Part 4	Original
4.1	The Schoolwide Enrichment Model	Published in *The Schoolwide Enrichment Model* published by Prufrock Press
4.2	The Enrichment Triad Model	Published in *The Schoolwide Enrichment Model* published by Prufrock Press

Figure	Title	Origination of figure
4.3	Sample of If I Ran the School	Published in *The Schoolwide Enrichment Model* published by Prufrock Press
4.4	Taxonomy of Type II Enrichment Processes	Published in *The Schoolwide Enrichment Model* published by Prufrock Press
5.1	Vehicles and Products for Type III Investigations	Published in *The Schoolwide Enrichment Model* published by Prufrock Press
5.2	Steps for Guiding Students through Independent and Self-Selected Projects	Original
5.3	Examples of Super Starter Projects	Original
6.1	An Action Model for Self-Determination	Permission included

Tables

Table	Title	Page #
1.1	Strengths Summary Sheet	Original
1.2	Summary Sheet: Engaging Stan	Original
1.3	Unit on the Middle Ages and the Feudal System	Original
2.1	Self-Regulation Strategies	Original
2.2	Common Attributes of Giftedness	Original
2.3	Characteristics of 2e Students	Original
3.1	Sample Enrichment Activity Student Log	Original
3.2	Simplified Enrichment Activity Student Log	Original
6.1	College Services Quiz	Original
6.2	The High School Day	Original
6.3	A Possible College Day	Original
6.4	A Sample Weekly Schedule	Original
6.5	What Types of Services Do You Use Now?	Original
6.6	Accommodations and Services Received in College	Original
6.7	What Services Might be Helpful in College	Original

Appendices

Appendix A	Developing Your Own Plan	Chapter 2, Original
Appendix B	Total Talent Portfolio	Published in *The Schoolwide Enrichment Model* published by Prufrock Press
Appendix C	If I Ran the School	Published in *The Schoolwide Enrichment Model* published by Prufrock Press
Appendix D	The Interest-A-Lyzer (Elementary and Secondary)	Published in *The Schoolwide Enrichment Model* published by Prufrock Press
Appendix E	Primary Interest-A-Lyzer	Published in *The Schoolwide Enrichment Model* published by Prufrock Press
Appendix F (p. 204)	Action Information Message	Published in *The Schoolwide Enrichment Model* published by Prufrock Press
Appendix G (p. 208)	Management Plan for Individual and Small Group Investigations	Published in *The Schoolwide Enrichment Model* published by Prufrock Press
Appendix H (p. 226)	College Services Quiz Answer Key	P. 51, Original

Contributors

Sally M. Reis holds the Letitia N. Morgan Chair in Educational Psychology, is a Board of Trustees Distinguished Professor, and is well known for her work with academically talented students. She was Principal Investigator for the National Research Center on the Gifted and Talented for 20 years and has authored or co-authored over 250 articles, books, book chapters, and technical reports. She is a past president of NAGC. Her research interests involve special populations of gifted and talented students, with a focus on learning-disabled students, gifted females, and diverse groups. She is also interested in extensions of the Schoolwide Enrichment Model for both gifted and talented students as a method to expand offerings and provide general enrichment to identify talents and potentials in students who have not been previously identified as gifted. She is the Co-Director of Confratute, the longest running summer institute in the development of gifts and talents. She has been a consultant to numerous schools and ministries of education throughout the U.S. and abroad and her work has been translated into several languages and widely used around the world.

Susan Baum, Ph.D. is an educator, author, consultant, Chancellor of Bridges Graduate School for Cognitive Diversity in Education and Director of the 2e Center for Research and Professional Development. The author of *To Be Gifted and Learning Disabled*, her writing and research covers many areas of education, including differentiated curriculum and instruction, gifted education, gifted learning-disabled students, and gifted underachieving students. Her work on twice-exceptional students is recognized globally and she has received many awards for her contributions to the field of twice exceptionality and strength-based, talent-focused teaching and learning.

Joseph Madaus, Ph.D. is a tenured professor and the Director of the Collaborative on Postsecondary Education and Disability in the Neag School of Education at UConn. He has been recognized for his service to the field of higher education and disability (American College Personnel Association [ACPA] award and Oliver P. Kolstoe Award for significant lifetime contributions to the field of career development and transition from Division on Career Development and Transition [DCDT]) and for his research (Distinguished Scholar award from Neag School of Education). He has over 110 articles published, in press, or in review in referred journals or textbook chapters on postsecondary education and students with disabilities. He is the co-editor of the *International Research Handbook on Higher Education and Disability* (with co-PI Dukes).

Nicholas Gelbar is a psychologist and researcher at the Neag School of Education at the University of Connecticut. He worked for over five years at the Autism Center at the Hospital for Special Care as a psychologist and is a nationally certified school psychologist as well as a board-certified Behavior Analyst at the Doctoral Level. He has training and expertise in identifying and teaching students identified as neurodiverse and twice-exceptional. He is the author of over 50 publications related to his areas of expertise.

Acknowledgments

We thank our colleagues, Julie Delgado, Allesandra Bergmark, and Rachael Desautel, for their helpful edits on earlier drafts of our manuscript. We thank the students, parents, and professionals who generously gave their time to share their experiences. Our work was guided by their insights and advice. We also acknowledge the many educators and parents who support talented students with disabilities across the world—may you always find time to focus on their strengths and interests.

Introduction

This publication serves as a practical guide designed for educators who work with gifted students with disabilities, also known as neurodiverse students. Our primary emphasis focuses on exploring how educators can implement an alternative pedagogical approach to effectively engage and assist students in achieving both academic and personal success. The authorship of this book includes contributors who hold diverse roles, including educators, psychologists, parents, and scholars. We have collaborated with educators and parents of these students for decades. In this book, we offer practical advice and easily implemented strategies for working with this population. We explore methods for providing various types of enrichment in the classroom, including ways of assessing and developing individual interests and promoting positive social and emotional well-being. While academic success can present difficulties for some neurodiverse students, we offer practical guidance and real-life examples from evidence-based research that demonstrate the high attainability of success for this population. Our primary objective is to offer comprehensive assistance and support to educators and parents in their efforts to guide students and children toward a successful transition into adulthood.

1

Using Strength-Based Pedagogy for Students with Disabilities

An Introduction and Overview of Strategies

When ten-year-old Stan proudly displayed the bench he built in his home workshop, no one could deny his extraordinary woodworking skills. Despite numerous frustrations, Stan had spent countless hours designing and carefully constructing the piece. Finally, after an incredible amount of work, the bench met his high standards. Over the course of the project, Stan had found solace and comfort in the workshop and viewed it as a place that would allow him to stay calm and be alone with his ideas (he even placed a sign on the door that read 'No Siblings Allowed'). Stan found that he liked to be completely engaged while working with no distractions. However, woodworking was not Stan's only area of interest. As a born naturalist and entrepreneur, Stan ran the school's chicken club, which he turned into a profitable egg business. Stan worked with his classmates to earn money for their horticulture project by creating a business that sold the herbal products they had grown. Stan dreamed of becoming an Eagle Scout and took on leadership roles whenever possible.

Given his strengths, it may come as a surprise that Stan struggled with the core curriculum in school. He had great difficulty with reading and communicating his ideas through writing.

DOI: 10.4324/9781003511861-1

He was highly anxious in the classroom and often refused to try anything he perceived as difficult, which led to him rarely completing assignments. Though Stan was academically gifted, he consistently underachieved. Stan is a child with dyslexia and perfectionism, also called a 'twice-exceptional' (2e) student.

Introduction

Joseph Renzulli's 1978 work introduced one of the most widely cited and well-known descriptions of giftedness. He explained that gifted behaviors emerge 'in certain people, at certain times, and under certain circumstances.' This concept, known as the three-ring conception of giftedness, emphasizes that **gifted behaviors** manifest when above-average ability, creativity, and task commitment intersect in a specific area of interest or talent.

You likely know students just like Stan. You may have noticed the ways that they demonstrate commitment and achievement in their areas of interest but fail to produce quality work in the classroom. You may have also noticed that conversations about these students often revolve around what these students *cannot* do. Discussions around this child likely begin from a place of deficit and end with a remediation plan that fails to include options that incorporate the child's interests or abilities into the classroom. Plans like the one above often fail to work, ending in frustration and disappointment for both the student and their teachers.

Recent evidence suggests that, when teaching strategies that incorporate individual strengths and learning preferences, students become more engaged, open to skill development, and involved in pathways that build positive peer relationships (Baum, Schader, and Hébert, 2014; Reis, Gelbar, and Madaus, 2021; Reis et al., 2022). Although this strength-based approach to teaching and learning is highly effective for all students, it is foundational and critically important for 2e students who simultaneously exhibit learning challenges and above-average abilities. In this chapter, we will introduce the ways we define, contextualize, and understand this type of student through a strength-based instructional approach.

Understanding the Twice-exceptional (2e) Student

An underserved and often overlooked population of bright, creative, neurodiverse students like Stan can be found in every classroom and school in the country. These students can become frustrated and bored with a prescribed curriculum that inadequately meets their needs, often leading to behaviors detrimental to their learning. Such students are typically considered to be twice-exceptional. Exceptionality refers to individuals who exhibit both high intellectual or creative abilities and one or more disabilities or learning challenges. Many different definitions of 2e exist, but generally students identified as 2e have academic talents and special abilities, as well as either attention deficit hyperactivity disorder (ADHD), autism spectrum disorder (ASD), and learning disability (LD; Foley Nicpon et al., 2011). And of course, some students identified as 2e have a combination of these and other challenges, too. Students with 2e may require individualized support in various areas including processing speed, executive functions, language skills, social interaction, adaptation, and psychosocial functioning (Assouline, Foley-Nicpon, and Dockery, 2012). Below, Figure 1.1 illustrates the many ways in which exceptionalities may combine. Each combination presents differently in the classroom and has varying impacts on a child's educational achievement. Regardless, intersecting combinations of traits can become problematic if they are not recognized, understood, and supported.

Identification of 2e Children

Most conversations concerning talented or high-potential students who are 2e begin with the challenging process of identification. Why is it difficult to identify 2e students and why is identification often delayed for this group? One reason is that, in some states, students must perform two or three grade levels below their chronological grade level to be eligible for special education services. This criterion fails 2e students who may be achieving at or slightly below grade level despite their high potential.

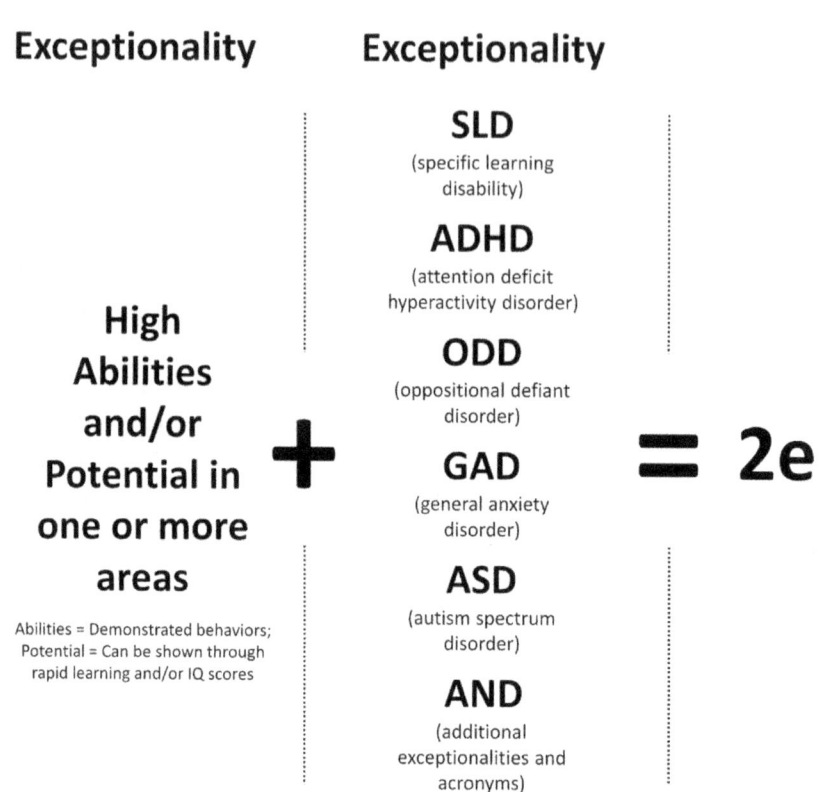

FIGURE 1.1 Combination of Exceptionalities (Schader and Baum, 2015)

Additionally, the disabilities of many 2e students only become more apparent as academic concepts increase in difficulty, making timely intervention impossible during many critical learning periods.

Furthermore, the lack of training for teachers and school psychologists related to 2e students contributes to their underidentification. Historically, school psychologists were trained primarily to identify differences between a student's intellectual capabilities and their actual performance only using standardized tests, such as aptitude tests or other forms of assessment. This methodology likely influenced the discrepancy formulas that are currently used to diagnose students who are 2e. For example, a discrepancy may exist between ability and achievement, with high scores in a performance area paired with low scores in a verbal area. School psychologists were often concerned exclusively with the large gaps demonstrated by some students with high abilities. However, fully understanding these discrepancies is complicated, and most researchers agree that singular scores should not be used as the sole determinant of whether someone is 2e (Baum et al., 1989; Hansford, 1987; Silverman, 1989). This leads to a need for further observation and evaluation which, considering the time and money it takes to administer assess students, can make identification of 2e students expensive.

Parents and teachers often notice characteristics of 2e before these students are formally recognized as 2e. Most students who are identified as 2e are identified at the middle or high school level, despite teachers' and parents' requests for testing and assistance in primary and elementary school (Reis, Gentry, and Maxfield, 1998). Although student learning problems are often evident to parents and teachers in early grades, research has shown most students referred at these ages are not identified as disabled until later in school. Why were they identified so much later? Often, the talents and abilities of gifted students mask their disabilities, and, in turn, their disabilities may mask their giftedness. Subsequently, many 2e students are excluded or underrepresented in both programs for disabled students and programs for gifted and talented students.

2e Students in the Classroom

Both 2e students and the adults who live with and teach them often find this group to be perplexing, as they have unique personal profiles that couple extraordinary abilities in some areas and debilitating deficits in others. As you have likely seen, assistance for these students tends to focus on their challenges, resulting in inconsistent support from adults and rigid goals with a focus on 'fixing' these students. The support plans that are developed for these students usually include strategies such as remediation of basic skills, social awareness classes, and behavioral interventions. What we will discuss in this book, however, is that **these students are not broken** and do not need to be 'fixed.' 2e students are quite capable of learning and typically have unique abilities that do not function best in a typical or vertical educational environment. Consider the following examples of learning behaviors described by educators that can frustrate and confuse the parents and teachers of 2e children (Baum and Schader, 2024; Reis, Gelbar, and Madaus, 2021):

- During classroom discussions, 2e students can contribute creative, insightful, and sophisticated ideas *BUT* they struggle to organize and express those ideas in written form.
- In areas of interest, 2e students can exhibit sustained engagement and commitment, *BUT* they cannot pay attention to tasks that lack novelty or sophistication or assignments that require significant listening and auditory processing.
- 2e students need intellectually challenging content *BUT* they have reading limitations or are slow processors.
- Many 2e students can have high personal standards for success *BUT* consistently produce sloppy and/or incomplete assignments.

When the deficits become the focus of attention in school, they overshadow the potential of these intellectually gifted and academically challenged youngsters. The 'buts,' in fact, may steer attention and services away from developing a student's abilities and instead direct teachers toward a 'fix-it' approach. Unfortunately, this is what happened to Stan. In prior schools, Stan was provided with interventions to remediate his areas of weakness and fix his problematic behaviors. There was little acknowledgment or attention given to his interests, talents, and areas of strength. In addition, the extra support in his areas of deficit in reading and writing frequently occurred after school, which left Stan with limited time to pursue his interests, stifling his ability to be fulfilled and enriched outside of the classroom. Even his parents questioned whether he should withdraw from boy scouts until his grades improved, despite the knowledge that becoming an Eagle Scout was Stan's dream and passion. He was not viewed by his classmates, teachers, or parents as a capable and creative kid. In short, when the focus was on what Stan could not do, he lost more and more academic and social confidence. The 'fix-it' approach was not working for Stan—nor does it work for other students with goals of long-term growth in social, emotional, and intellectual development. In fact, this deficit-focused approach is being challenged considering the neurodiversity movement and breakthroughs in positive psychology (Seligman and Csikszentmihalyi, 2000; Silberman, 2015).

Neurodivergence

It is important to keep in mind that individuals with learning challenges experience additional invisible challenges beyond their primary disability. The Cleveland Clinic (2022) describes people whose brains are wired differently as *neurodivergent*. The concept of neurodivergence suggests that the strengths and challenges of these individuals are different but equally valid compared to neurotypical people. These differences should not be seen as deficits but as normal variations of brain functions that are incredibly valuable (Armstrong, 2010). Instead of focusing on what is wrong with how a neurodivergent brain works, modern psychologists are arguing for a strength-based approach.

Contrary to popular belief, the idea of capitalizing on an individual's strengths is not new. In the 1960s, while working at the University of Nebraska, psychology professor Donald Clifton boldly asked, 'What will happen when we think about what is right with people rather than fixating on what is wrong with them?' Clifton dedicated his career to researching and teaching human development. His goal was to demonstrate the true value of people developing their innate talents and strengths in ways that led to productive lives and improved well-being. His research resulted in a shift in how organizations functioned. Instead of providing specific training to employees with limited traditional abilities, organizations began identifying and using the unique talents of their employees. This approach led to the creation of diverse teams where individuals could harness their personal strengths. This practice of diversifying talents within an organization led to the development of leaders with different gifts, resulting in higher productivity and an increased sense of harmony within the institution.

Around the same time, Martin Seligman, a psychologist and professor at the University of Pennsylvania, advocated for shifting the focus from what people could *not* do to what they *could* do. He promoted the identification of factors that enhance people's emotional quality of life, in turn creating an approach that could improve overall well-being. In his inaugural speech as president of the American Psychological Association, Seligman (1999) argued that psychologists needed to study what makes happy people happy, noting

> The most important thing, the most general thing I learned, was that psychology was half-baked, literally half-baked. We had baked the part about mental illness . . . The other side's unbaked, the side of strength, the side of what we're good at.

Recognizing the potential of this approach, many practitioners in psychology, social work, and education began incorporating the principles of positive psychology into their practice. Positive psychology, often defined as the study of well-being and the positive attributes of life, focuses on gaining satisfaction and understanding in order to be content and happy in life. To test the theories of this pedagogy, Sin and Lyubomirsky (2009) conducted a meta-analysis of 51 interventions involving 4,266 individuals. The results showed that positive psychology interventions significantly enhanced individual well-being and reduced rates of depression in patients.

You might be wondering how all of this applies to the field of education and, more importantly, to your classroom. While the actions of Clifton and Seligman gained widespread recognition, a smaller yet equally significant positive psychology movement in the field of education was driven by research in gifted and talented education. This research has shown the positive effects of educational enrichment and talent development, particularly for reversing underachievement, building self-efficacy, and improving self-esteem among bright students with disabilities (Baum, Cooper, and Neu, 2001; Baum and Schader, 2018; Reis et al., 2022; Renzulli and Reis, 2014). Despite the strong evidence supporting a strength-based approach, special education practices have been slow to change. Most special educators still rely on a deficit-based ('fix-it') model as seen in many Individual Educational Plan (IEP) forms. These forms briefly mention student strengths but do not require the integration of personal abilities and talents into the plan. While IEPs do identify cognitive strengths, up to now, they have not sufficiently described or measured the use of strengths, enrichment, and talent development to promote student growth.

Fortunately, a shift is happening. With the advent of approaches such as Universal Design for Learning (UDL), there is growing interest in engaging students through strength-based and talent-focused services. Teachers and educational researchers must work together to highlight the remarkable attributes that 2e students display. As educators, we understand that 2e students need a learning environment filled with adults who recognize and value cognitive diversity and who will create opportunities that reflect what these students can do while looking ahead to who they will become. By reading this book and implementing some of the recommended practices in your classroom, you are actively challenging the 'fix-it' approach and demonstrating that you value your students' strengths!

Strength-Based, Talent-Focused Model of Teaching and Learning: How Do We Do It?

To begin, it is essential to create learning environments that allow every student to work in areas of interest and take pride in their achievements. We must remember that 2e students need sophisticated experiences that satiate their curiosity in ways that align with their specific type of neurodivergence. In a strength-based approach, we recommend using four specific strategies to develop the talents of these students (Baum, Schader, and Hébert, 2014). These strategies include: a) engaging through strengths, b) leveraging strengths, c) dual differentiation, and d) enrichment and talent development opportunities. In this and the following chapters, we will describe these categories in greater depth.

The Foundation: Getting to Know Your Students

Simply put, knowing your students means becoming more curious about student interests, learning preferences, personality profiles, experiences, and talents. While we focus on this process in subsequent chapters, it is important to understand that this knowledge includes an awareness of the ways brains are wired and the circumstances under which students perform at their personal best. Such information informs the creation of 2e-friendly environments and the implementation of a strength-based curriculum and instruction that benefit all students.

The process of knowing your students involves more than sending out interest surveys; discovering a student's strengths is an ongoing process that takes time. Understanding the children in your classroom requires a genuine curiosity about their interests and hobbies, including the activities they do outside of school, when they feel in 'flow,' and what brings them satisfaction. We define flow as a deeply engaging learning experience where students are absorbed in work they find enjoyable. The ultimate goal of strength-based learning is to discover when and where all students are at their personal best, which is especially important for those identified as 2e who may otherwise struggle in school.

Consider the following: What are your students doing for fun? What are they producing in school? When are they willing to stay in the struggle and engage in the work of learning new things? How are their talents identified? In short, what are the circumstances that feed into the student's intrinsic motivation to succeed?

Adopting a philosophy of strength-based, talent-focused teaching and learning requires teachers to know their students well. Teachers can develop their skills in integrating and incorporating information about students' interests, talents, and preferences into curriculum planning. Unfortunately, many educators talk about promoting a strength-based approach but struggle to demonstrate how and where that happens. Although caring teachers may have the will, they may not have the ways (or the skills) to make it happen. In this book, we aim to explain how strength-based instructional strategies operate within a classroom setting and how these strategies impact 2e learners.

A summary of the information learned about Stan is organized in the Strengths Summary Sheet in Table 1.1 below. This sheet highlights Stan's traits and the activities he enjoys. Summary sheets like the one provided may be useful when designing strength-based activities for students like Stan.

Table 1.1 Strengths Summary Sheet

Taking stock
This student (Stan) . . .

Has dyslexic brain wiring, which for him translates into preferences for hands-on activities, creative problem-solving, and spatial engineering activities.

Interests
- is passionate about building
- has enthusiasm for gourmet cooking
- loves nature
- involved in boy scouts
- is curious about how things work, especially mechanically
- is entrepreneurial

Learning and personality preferences
- shows leadership ability
- is primarily a creative problem solver/practical manager
- prefers non- fiction books
- enjoys graphic novels

Stan thrives when working with adults and is at his best when alone in his well-equipped workshop, creating carpentry products.

Source: Baum and Schader, 2024

Creating 2e Friendly Environments

As we know from biodiversity, an organism's environment is critical in either supporting or hindering its growth. Organisms use a concept called positive niche construction, where they either build what they need in their environment to survive or find a new environment that best suits their needs. Thomas Armstrong (2010) adapted this idea for education to describe a process through which parents, teachers, mental health professionals, and neurodivergent individuals can modify their environments to ensure success in school, work, and life. To create the best learning conditions for 2e students, the five key elements of a positive learning environment need to be considered.

Aspects of Environment

We can view the environment as the setting and surroundings of a student's educational journey (Baum and Novak, 2010). The underlying question is what environmental conditions will encourage and support successful learning and growth in the following five components (Baum et al. 2017; Schader & Baum, 2015):

- ◆ **The physical environment** encompasses the conditions that allow students to regulate their physical needs. The physical environment provides the basis for a healthy and happy learning space. Consider lighting, space for movement, or sensory spaces to limit physical stressors for your students.
- ◆ **The academic/intellectual environment** refers to the aspects of a learning setting that cater to the cognitive and intellectual needs of students. This part of a child's experience can be tricky to think about because, while 2e students are exceptionally bright, their academic progress can be uneven, causing their needs to be overlooked. Consider what content a child is learning, the pace of their learning, and the level of novelty in their curriculum.

- **The social environment** describes the aspects of a learning setting that influence students' interactions, relationships, and sense of belonging. It is critical that they have opportunities to spend time with people they can relate to, including interest-peers of all ages. This happens best in settings when students are allowed to collaborate with others who share similar 'enthusiasms.' Consider groupings, pairings, and relationships when designing assignments.
- **The emotional environment** refers to the parts of a classroom or school that affect students' emotional well-being and psychological safety. This area must be carefully considered as 2e students will not be able to learn unless they feel psychologically safe. Negative behaviors must be viewed first as potential indicators of anxiety, not simply addressed with disciplinary consequences. Think about stress triggers, such as too much noise in the classroom, or emotional triggers, such as difficult content, that might impact your student.
- **The creative environment** encompasses the aspects of a learning environment that encourage and support creativity, innovation, and divergent thinking. A positive creative environment involves providing accessible materials and designing assignments that allow sufficient time for exploration while respecting a student's unique way of working. Consider incorporating arts and makerspaces, project-based learning, and innovation labs into the larger school environment.

Component One: The Physical Environment

Depending on the types of neurodiversities involved, physical environments can be particularly challenging for students with sensory or movement issues. A student's ability to concentrate and produce can be significantly hindered when their physical needs are ignored or overlooked. Although you cannot change the shape or location of your classroom, there are key elements of the physical environment that can be altered to support the growth of 2e students. When designing the ideal classroom, we want to consider elements like the furniture in the room, the lighting features, the accessibility of the spaces provided, as well as the equipment and organization of activities.

Students with ADHD need a physical environment that allows for movement, such as rocking chairs, standing podiums for lessons or seat work, and instruction that incorporates movement. For example, a 'thinking lane' around the perimeter of the classroom can stimulate the writing process by allowing students to work out ideas while completing laps.

Alternatively, students with ASD benefit from environments in which there are quiet spaces. This includes classroom areas that allow them to shut out excessive stimuli, sensory spaces outside the classroom for self-regulation, and access to noise-canceling headphones. These students may also do well with fidgets or places to move to focus their energy.

Students with a specific learning disability (SLD), like Stan, often benefit from supplementary resources that provide visual or auditory information in addition to written language. Websites, video clips, podcasts, audiobooks, and graphic novels help these students learn in ways that do not focus solely on written words. They also benefit from access to materials that encourage individual productivity, including art and building supplies, computer programs for film making, and stage-like spaces.

Component Two: The Academic/Intellectual Environment

2e students require an academic environment that engages their intellect, specific interests, and talents. When designing an academic or intellectual environment for 2e students, educators need to consider their intellectual abilities. Before beginning a unit or new part of the curriculum, it is helpful to pretest these students to ensure that they are being adequately challenged. Lessons should engage them in critical and creative thinking through pertinent and provocative topics, as these students thrive when they can talk with experts and engage in intellectual sparring. Extracurricular activities might include competitions, contests, and opportunities to engage with other students with similar abilities and interests. Alternatively, if your school is unable to provide engaging challenges for these students, access to online college courses or community college classes could be compelling options.

It is important to understand that while all bright students respond well to a captivating curriculum, 2e students with ADHD often have significantly higher rates of focus when presented with stimulating material. As William Dodson (2023) explains, people with ADHD have an interest-based nervous system that responds best to novelty, challenge, and short-term assignments rather than long-range projects. This suggests that classrooms providing engaging material are more likely to help 2e students meet their academic potential.

For students with ASD, the academic environment needs to be structured and predictable to reduce anxiety and enhance learning. These students benefit from clear, concise instructions and factually based assignments that allow them to increase their knowledge and expertise in an area. Incorporating their special interests into the curriculum can significantly enhance their engagement and motivation. For instance, a student fascinated by dinosaurs might thrive on assignments that incorporate paleontology themes.

For students with SLD, it is important to meet their intellectual needs in ways that engage their minds without taxing their lagging academic skills. When Stan's 6th-grade class was tasked with creating a model of a bridge using toothpicks and glue, he was frustrated. Having constructed bridges since preschool, he cringed at the assignment for this physics unit. Sensing his frustration, his teacher asked if he had a different model he would prefer building. Stan chose to design a stadium to scale using wood, a project more suited to his skills and interest level. He showed high levels of creativity and task commitment as he pushed himself in novel ways. By the end of the assignment, Stan had learned much more about the principles of physics than he would have if he had been required to rehearse mastered skills with the original bridge construction project.

Component Three: The Social Environment

It is very important to consider the social aspects of a 2e student's experience. Because of their differences, they can be bullied, teased, or shunned, leading to heightened stress and anxiety. Some 2e students have difficulty forming relationships in a traditional classroom and school setting, which leaves them feeling isolated and alone. How the teacher arranges social interactions in the classroom can result in a student experiencing feelings of belonging or suffering from feelings of ostracism. When designing small groups, it is helpful to remember that relationships are best formed when individuals have things in common. Shared interests, goals, experiences, or abilities are likely to be a strong starting point for teamwork. Teachers can take advantage of this by matching student interests in group activities. For example, within a unit on the solar system, students could be allowed to choose a topic to research and present to the class. Topics could range from a planet's atmospheric conditions and weather to specific geological features of a given system. By encouraging students to choose their topic and bond through shared interests, teachers can create a highly positive social environment for students of all abilities. It is important to remember that these students' interests rather than their age are the best contributors to forming relationships.

Most 2e students benefit from connecting virtually. Participating with a group of peers playing computer games is a beneficial method for forming friendships among 2e students. Structures like this allow students to control the amount of time they spend in social interaction while bonding them through shared contributions. These relationships then spill over to other activities and open doors to additional social avenues. A teacher might take advantage of these potential connections by encouraging these students to join an after-school computer or Dungeons and Dragons club.

Students with ADHD often face social challenges due to their impulsivity, hyperactivity, and difficulty sustaining attention. These traits can lead to misunderstandings and conflicts with peers. To support the social development of students with

ADHD, it is essential to create structured opportunities for positive social interactions. Teachers can design activities that allow for movement and frequent breaks, which helps these students manage their energy and focus. Group projects that incorporate hands-on tasks and clear, concise roles can facilitate better collaboration and reduce frustration. Additionally, pairing students with ADHD with understanding and patient peers can help build strong friendships.

Students with ASD often experience difficulties in social interactions due to challenges in communication and social understanding. To support the social development of these 2e students, it is important to create an environment that provides clear social expectations and routines. Incorporating interest-based activities can help students with ASD connect with peers who share similar passions. For instance, a teacher could organize a robotics club or an art group, which would allow students to bond over common interests and develop meaningful relationships. Within these interest group settings, students can be reminded of social protocols that allow them to engage productively.

Students with SLD often struggle with academic tasks, which can affect their self-esteem and social interactions. These students may feel embarrassed or self-conscious about their difficulties, leading to social withdrawal or isolation. To support the social development of students with SLD, teachers can create an environment that emphasizes strengths and promotes self-confidence. This can be done by designing group activities that allow students to showcase their talents and abilities, such as art projects, drama performances, or science experiments. Providing positive reinforcement and celebrating small achievements can continue to boost student confidence and encourage participation.

In the case of Stan, he typically preferred activities he could do independently. His most comfortable relationships were with adults who served a mentorship role. At one point, Stan had the opportunity to work with a teacher to write a successful grant to bring box turtles into the classroom. During this time, Stan opened up to his teacher about his hopes and dreams and now, years later, they still stay in touch. For Stan, relationships proved to work best when they were focused, natural, and purposeful.

Component Four: The Emotional Environment

2e students frequently lack skills for self-regulation, organization, and conflict management. They can be easily overwhelmed by negativity or excessive demands and struggle to handle behavioral expectations that fall outside of their innate skill set. For example, a 2e student might become overstimulated by the noise within a classroom, making it difficult for them to complete an assignment. Outside of the classroom, schoolwide policies regarding attendance, scheduling, grading, and homework can be problematic for these students, as they need to feel psychologically safe to regulate and manage their emotions. Supporting these students might involve taking a flexible approach and including their voices in finding solutions for schoolwide expectations.

Students with ADHD usually focus and engage best when learning is active, and assignments provide broad boundaries within which their creative minds can explore. Adult tolerance for humor (sometimes irreverent) and respect for their often out-of-the-box thinking can build trust, creating a psychologically safe environment for these students. Teachers can also work to be supportive and compassionate toward these students when they get overwhelmed or overstimulated in the classroom.

Students with ASD often benefit from authentic opportunities to practice social awareness and skills. These instances might occur during field trips, interviews, and other 'real world' activities, where students feel less pressure to mask and conform to a rigid social structure that has been established within a classroom. Structured programs for decision-making, such as Creative Problem Solving (CPS), enable these students to generate alternatives and gain perspective on the ideas of others. Often, these students need explicit social cues that are critically important for social skill-building. Much like their peers with ADHD, tolerance and respect from teachers and peers can lead to an understanding of their tendency for black-and-white thinking and their unabashed honesty.

Students with SLD often feel emotionally supported when creative thinking is encouraged, and their expertise is acknowledged and valued as they see the big picture and explain the world metaphorically. They function best when teachers don't place a premium on using reading and writing but instead offer options for students to communicate what they have learned in different ways.

Students like Stan often feel overwhelmed by homework, as they are required to exert a significant amount of mental labor to understand basic aspects of an assignment. Stan's anxiety manifested in procrastination, leading him to fail to submit homework and watch as the amount of make-up work became insurmountable. His high school's policy on homework did not seem workable for students like Stan, whose learning was compromised and whose anxiety levels could quickly paralyze production. Stan talked to his advisor about his growing discomfort with school. An examination of the policies revealed that homework was being graded and weighted at 25% of a student's final course grade. One successful idea that has been implemented in one public high school for gifted and high-ability students (many of whom were 2e) was to enable students to decide the weight of their assignments toward their course grades. If this does not feel plausible, you may want to give students more choices in how they show mastery of content within their courses.

Component Five: The Creative Environment

Too often and in too many schools, opportunities for creative thinking and originality have been diminished as the emphasis on inflexible standards and higher test scores has increased. It is not uncommon for 2e students to have the correct answer but be unable to show or explain it in traditional ways. Systems that do not allow for inventive problem-solving effectively punish creative 2e students. These students love to entertain 'what if' ideas and enjoy exploring different possible solutions to a given problem. They find joy in being funny, making puns, and being silly, which may disrupt the typical classroom. However, many of these students display disruptive behavior as a way of expressing creativity while deflecting attention to survive in a system that rarely works for them. To support these students, it is important to appreciate the role of creativity and play in learning as they begin their quests to be unique. Many students who are 2e would rather find ten different ways to solve one math problem than do ten math problems using the taught algorithm. These students often excel when given open-ended assignments that encourage all forms of expression. Tasks like these can enable teachers to get an accurate measure of what a student knows or doesn't know.

Students with ADHD often exhibit high levels of creativity and out-of-the-box thinking but may struggle in traditional classroom settings due to their need for movement and stimulation. They can be impulsive and easily distracted, which can lead to disruptions. To support these students, it is crucial to provide opportunities for active learning and incorporate movement into lessons. Allowing them to work on open-ended projects that align with their interests can help maintain their focus and engagement. Incorporate 'what if' thinking and encourage them to find new ways to solve problems.

Similarly, students with ASD have unique perspectives and strong interests in specific topics, which drives their creativity. However, they may face challenges with social interactions and rigid classroom structures. To support these students, it is important to create a structured and predictable environment while allowing for flexibility in how they express their creativity. Providing clear instructions and visual support can help them navigate open-ended assignments. Encouraging their special interests and integrating them into the curriculum can improve their engagement and allow them to showcase their strengths in innovative ways.

Students with SLD may struggle with traditional academic tasks but possess creative problem-solving abilities and strengths in areas not typically assessed by standard tests. To support these students, teachers should offer multiple ways for them to demonstrate their understanding and knowledge. Open-ended assignments and projects that allow for creativity and choice can enable students with SLD to leverage their strengths and minimize their challenges. By creating a supportive environment that values diverse talents, celebrates innovative thinking, and provides alternative assessment methods, educators can help these students excel and fully participate in their learning.

It may also be helpful to encourage creative thinking with physical resources. For Stan, it was essential to have the equipment, materials, and tools he needed to complete projects. When he was building the habitat for the turtles, he requested a budget so he could make his shopping list. He found the best prices and found innovative ways to stretch that budget. This project allowed him to express his creativity while simultaneously supporting his classroom community.

Strength-Based Pedagogy: Designing Curriculum with the Student in Mind

Overview of Key Instructional Strategies

Once information is collected and learning environments are created with options that meet student needs, instructional planning and implementation can begin. For strength-based pedagogy to be effective, instructional design must be purposeful, which includes identifying the 'why' or 'to what end' of a particular lesson. The following tenets of strengths-based systems developed and tested at Bridges Academy described by Luscher et al. (2021) can help guide your own teaching and learning practices.

Engaging Students in Learning

Too often we walk into classrooms to find students with their heads on their desks and hoodies hiding their faces. Many appear to be disengaged from the classroom, the school, and their peers. One easy way to stimulate engagement is to incorporate relevant interests through varied learning experiences, resources, and choices within any unit of study. This improves the probability that neurodiverse students will actively participate during class and have a productive learning experience. In Figure 1.2, depicted below, you can see the types of activities, resources, and projects that invite students of all abilities to learn.

> **Engaging a student through strengths:**
>
> **What kinds of activities, resources, and projects did I include in my unit that would invite this student to learn?**
>
> **What is it?**
> - The creation of curricular units that invite engagement and production through strength-based choices to relate to the student's profile and connect to the learning outcomes.
>
> **Background thinking:**
> - If students have sufficient opportunity to engage in the topic, process information, and communicate learning in ways that align to their unique brain wiring, learning preferences, interests, and talent they would be more willing to participate and produce even if some activities are difficult for them.
>
> **Outcome:**
> - Mastery of the unit's objectives.

FIGURE 1.2 Engaging Students through Strengths (Baum and Schader, 2023)

To further understand how to use strengths for engagement, we can return to Stan. The summary sheet in Table 1.2 below shows curricular implications for addressing Stan's areas of interests, abilities, and talents. By understanding and incorporating Stan's interests and learning preferences, we can create plans for particular strategies and activities that keep Stan fully engaged. Table 1.2 below lists possible ways to engage students like Stan. Sheets like this can be a helpful ongoing reference tool throughout the year.

By filling out and updating these types of 'Summary Sheets' for individual 2e students, educators can develop alternative ideas for teaching any curriculum unit. For example, when Stan was in sixth grade, his humanities teacher was concerned that he might not be interested in the upcoming Middle Ages unit and could find some of the reading and writing assignments difficult. She reviewed the unit goals, lessons, and project options she had planned and then consulted Stan's 'Summary Sheet' to determine how Sam's strengths would be supported by her what she had originally planned. Knowing that other students had similar learning profiles, she realized that any additional modifications to the unit could benefit those students as well.

Her assessment revealed that the Middle Ages unit plan, with its focus on the economic advantages of the feudal system,

Table 1.2 Summary Sheet: Engaging Stan

If we know . . .	*Then consider . . .*
Stan is dyslexic, has specific challenges with reading and writing. His strengths lie in his creativity and special thinking. Stan reports that he prefers hands-on activities.	♦ Using resources that feature more visuals and less text, such as graphic novels, magazines, video clips, etc. ♦ Using graphic organizers. ♦ Offering creative, open-ended assignments. ♦ Providing access to Maker Space, tools, and project-based learning.
Stan likes: ♦ Nature ♦ Building ♦ Cooking ♦ Taking new ideas and making them into a business ♦ Being in charge ♦ Working with adults	♦ Introducing outdoor activities that involve observation and environmental experiences. ♦ Relating environmental studies to a topic at hand. ♦ Including project choices around inventing, building, or engineering. ♦ Integrating cooking, authentically if possible. ♦ Connecting lessons to entrepreneurial activities such as think tanks and start-ups. ♦ Assigning as group project leader. ♦ Finding opportunities to interview experts about topics within the unit—look for mentoring opportunities.

would be of interest to Stan. However, she recognized that her plan could be enriched to address Stan's interests and talents and encourage students to engage with that material. She suggested that her students think outside the box for their assignments. Stan's love of cooking could lead him to conduct historical research into medieval banquets and learn how they were prepared. Alternatively, Stan might want to be in charge of staging such an event, including menu planning, cooking, and serving, which would place him in a leadership role. By providing a variety of options, Stan's teacher created a more engaging assignment that supported each student's individual growth.

In addition to the main assignment, Stan's teacher designed a trebuchet competition for her class. She determined that Stan's passion and skills in construction aligned well with this activity and chose to make Stan a team captain to build his confidence and leadership skills. Finally, she reviewed the resources offered within the unit to ensure that new information was accessible to her class without forcing them to do extensive reading. The unit plan in Table 1.3 below shows the additions she made to the unit to boost student engagement and productivity.

Table 1.3 Unit on the Middle Ages and the Feudal System

Standards addressed in unit

Credibility of primary and secondary sources, drawing related conclusions from information learned.

Interpretations of history are subject to change as new information is uncovered.

Basic indicators of societal performance, conduct cost-benefit analyses of economic and political issues.

Unit topics
  Nature of the Feudal System—advantages and disadvantages
  The role of guilds in the economic development
  Art and architecture of the period
  The cause and effect of the Crusades games

Added—Life in the Middle Ages: Medieval feasts.

Resources with Stan in mind:

Overview of the Middle Ages includes rich visuals, timelines, and video clips. https://nsms6thgradesocialstudies.weebly.com/middle-ages.html

Learning activities with Stan in mind

Read a picture book that describes the preparation and celebration of a medieval feast for royal guests held at an English manor house.

Assess the historical accuracy of the information, especially regarding the foods served at the feast.

Prepare foods for a class banquet using historically accurate recipes.

Projects with Stan in mind

Trebuchet Games competition—Encourage Stan to be leader of his team. Students form teams that will design, construct, and test trebuchets to compete for a prize. The focus of the activity is for students to be able to work as a group while investigating force and motion. Everyone on the team will have specific tasks they must complete to be successful in the competition.

Leveraging Strengths for Skill Development

Once we know the different strengths of students in our classroom, we can leverage them to address areas of improvement. Typically, 2e students' learning challenges show up in specific conceptual areas where verbal or numerical skills are required. But they may understand the concept in another form of expression, for instance through images, music, or movement.

Suppose a student is having difficulty understanding how to graph data but is talented in music. Think about possible connections between music and the concept of graphing. The musical staff is a graph depicting how sounds go from low to high to create a melody or tune. Bar graphs and line graphs also use 'up and down' as a symbol structure. Starting a discussion on graphing by playing or singing musical notes as a scale can demonstrate the use of high and low quantities. As we have learned from Piaget, learning happens when you can relate new information to something already known.

We can consider this in the context of a 2e student who was a highly talented musician but struggled with reading fluency. This student explained how he used music to improve his reading: 'I can't just sound out the words, the letters blend together like the notes on a page. When I discovered the connection to music, I figured out how to read better.' These types of simple examples remind us that our brains work best when we learn through an area of strength, where our brains can contextualize the task requirements. If a student understands a concept by using a musical symbol system, then this knowledge can be extended to other symbol systems such as numbers and words. Below, Figure 1.3 provides a summary of the ways that we can leverage strengths for skill development.

This style of teaching is especially beneficial for 2e students like Stan, whose dyslexia caused him to have difficulty with written expression. This proved to be pertinent when he was assigned a creative writing task. Stan struggled with the assignment, as he had significant difficulty with executive function, like poor organization and slow working memory, as he attempted to get his words on paper. Executive function includes the skills a student

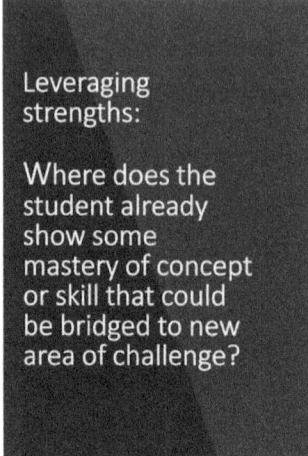

FIGURE 1.3 Leveraging Strengths (Baum and Schader, 2023)

has to direct behaviors such as making plans, organizing, getting started on work, and setting goals for completing projects and daily tasks. Often described by teachers and kids as brain skills, executive function helps students pay attention, identify steps to finish a task, organize, control impulses, and monitor one's performance and work output.

Stan is highly creative and loves fashioning projects with wood or experimenting with his own recipes in cooking. As a practical and linear thinker, Stan must have his own method of creating. In fact, his fifth-grade teacher, knowing this, simply asked him: 'Stan, how do you get ideas when you are crafting projects or inventing new recipes?' Stan thought for a moment and then, with a smile, replied, 'I see it in my head. When I can visualize the final project, I can break it down into steps. And once I get the steps in my head, I start to add more ideas as I go along.'

Could this method of working step-by-step be applied to his writing? Could he, in fact, build or craft his story? This might occur in a classroom where he could use Lego to build the setting and characters while adding the plot as he goes along. With this approach, Stan could create storyboards or use flow charts as visual guides to translate his ideas into written work. Strategies like these can be helpful for many students with 2e brain wiring.

Dual Differentiation
Strength-based instruction also incorporates the idea of dual differentiation. As we have mentioned, 2e students respond best to work that stimulates their intellect. They must be allowed to circumvent or tackle any challenges that may hamper their learning. Because of this, dual differentiation is a life- and learning-saver for these students (and their teachers). Consider how reading material can be advanced (differentiation #1) and, at the same time, work with poor decoding skills (differentiation #2). This approach helps to nurture the student's advanced abilities while helping them avoid roadblocks that limit their success.

We should treat 2e students who are already struggling in school the same way we treat students who are excelling and need less introductory instruction. The minds of 2e students crave complex, novel information and are resistant to redundant and simplistic learning. These children have difficulty with things that might be perceived as simple, like memorizing math facts, following directions, and using proper spelling while writing. Difficulty with decoding skills, for instance, might force highly verbal students to read material below their interest level because the vocabulary is more accessible. Many talented 2e students report that they are humiliated by watered-down curricula that match their perceived abilities but do not stimulate or encourage their learning.

Dually differentiated instruction uses a student's advanced abilities to sidestep learning challenges until the discrepancy between what they can and cannot do is greatly diminished. This idea is summarized in Figure 1.4 above. Essentially, we want to provide students with material that builds their confidence, encourages growth, and avoids their skill deficits. In practice, we

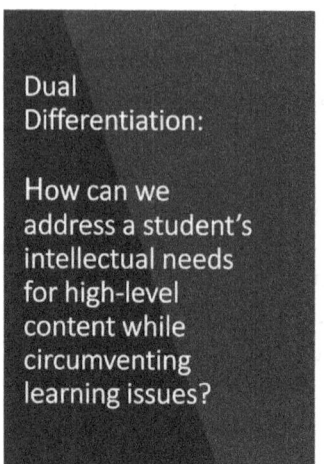

FIGURE 1.4 Dual Differentiation (Baum and Schader, 2023)

can look again to students like Stan, whose high verbal abilities and intellectual curiosity mirror that of older students, yet his decoding abilities are considerably below grade level. For him to improve engage conceptually, the content should be both easily decodable and intellectually engaging. Forms of writing like poetry can be wonderful for teaching with dual differentiation. Consider Robert Frost's *Stopping by Woods*—the words are simple and phonetic while the concept is abstract and meaningful. Let's look at the first two verses.

> *Whose woods are these I think I know.*
> *His house is in the village though;*
> *He will not see me stopping here*
> *To watch his woods fill up with snow.*
> *My little horse must think it queer*
> *To stop without a farmhouse near*
> *Between the woods and frozen lake*
> *The darkest evening of the year.*

For a 2e child, the format of poetry may be perceptually pleasing and relatively easy to read, and for a bright, curious mind, the content is intriguing. At Stan's school, the reading specialist used dual differentiation to support both Stan's reading fluency and comprehension. Because Stan was so interested in building and engineering, she gave him technical manuals replete with illustrations and diagrams. The short descriptions and pictures with captions contained vocabulary that was familiar to him. This not only intrinsically motivated Stan to read over the manuals but supported his growth in decoding. For students with 2e, it may be as simple as providing appropriate resources that are personally interesting and academically appropriate.

Enrichment and Talent Development

In our quest to support 2e students, we often forget the important role of intrinsic motivation. Intrinsic motivation refers to the drive to engage in an activity for its own sake because it is interesting, enjoyable, or satisfying rather than for some external reward or pressure. When a person is intrinsically motivated, they undertake a task because they find it inherently rewarding, rather than because they expect to receive something in return or to avoid a negative outcome. This type of motivation encourages 2e students to aim for success, develop their abilities, and grow their skills. Over the years, we have observed that the highest level of 2e teaching and learning is through enrichment and talent development, which we discuss in depth in subsequent chapters. Enrichment opportunities must be regarded as essential aspects of educational programming. During enrichment opportunities, students are typically motivated and goal-directed. They are more receptive to instruction and feedback, more likely to take positive risks, and more able to ask for the support they need. Even though students with 2e often struggle with executive function skills and social development, we often see change when students can engage in areas of 'infatuation' and high interest. When this happens, students increase their ability to manage their behaviors in the classroom. Enrichment and authentic talent development opportunities offer strength-based pathways to success that make sense and are satisfying for students. In this form of instruction, students use their own passions to fuel their willingness to overcome challenges.

Even more importantly, the future success of these students will depend upon how well they have been able to develop these interests and skills. Schools can support students by creating individual talent plans that will lead a student from novice, introductory experiences to those that approach levels of expertise. In the chapters to come, we will discuss various types of enrichment that can be critical for the development of our students. In Figure 1.5 below, you will find a basic description of enrichment and talent development opportunities.

Let's look at an example of a talent development opportunity (TDO) that will help us foreshadow other chapters in this book. A teacher wants to support the talent development of a 2e student, so she suggests the formation of a robotics club. The teacher knows that competition and extracurricular

| Enrichment and Talent Development Opportunities (TDOs): What opportunities are available to grow a student's talents and interests? | **What is it?**
• These are opportunities in which students can develop skills in areas of talents and interests as they purposefully grow from novice to expert in particular areas. These authentic learning experiences align to their areas of talents and interests.
Background thinking:
• When students work in a self-selected pursuit of a goal, there is high motivation to achieve their vision. During these times students are receptive to learning skills that help them overcome obstacles such as time management (meeting deadlines) or writing (a business plan).
Outcome:
• Development of skills toward experience. |

FIGURE 1.5 Enrichment and Talent Development Opportunities (Baum and Schader, 2023)

activities can be pathways to talent development, so the club is designed to engage in local competition with other schools. In order to compete, the students must form their teams, fundraise, and design their team brand. The competition has firm rules, time limits, and resources, all of which are used by the team to build industrial-size robots. The students then use their robots to play through an obstacle course. Students were asked to submit a safety video, produce a written plan, and meet specific deadlines. Tasks like these are often difficult for 2e students who are not inherently drawn to writing or attuned to time management. However, when these requirements are part of the competition, they find ways to meet these challenges. Several benefits of participating on the team are captured in this account of a March 2024 event, published in a school newspaper:

> Robotics Team 4019 'Mechanical Paradise' got tropical at the Ventura County Regional Competition this past weekend! The international FIRST event had our little-team-that-could pitted against juggernauts from China, Holland and Hawaii, as well as local favorites. Our team put in the hours this season and it showed. Our robot, affectionately named, 'AQ34', fought hard and was competitive against the best teams each match, and we ended up with a winning record and ranked in the middle of the pack by the end of the grueling but fun competition. Team 4019 never gave up, were gritty and resourceful with any issue that arose, and they were all very proud to have fought the good fight against some of the best teams in the world.
>
> (High School, 2024)

Let's think through another example. As this chapter opened, you were introduced to Stan, a young naturalist with entrepreneurial skills. As Stan grew, he not only became an engaged student, but he became a leader and a role model for others. The early 'hooks' that enticed him into learning and producing were the experiences that began outside of the core curriculum. If you'll remember, Stan's school had a chicken club and there was a horticulture enrichment cluster in which Stan did his best writing. When a horticulture enrichment opportunity called an enrichment cluster (see Chapter 4) was offered, Stan could not wait to sign up. The group grew herbs and learned to make skin care products. This interest in plants led the group to create a butterfly garden for the school grounds. As they began, Stan quickly realized that the group would need to raise funds if they were going to create the garden. He suggested to his cluster mates that they might want to sell the skin care products they had made. His peers loved the idea, so Stan organized the larger group into smaller teams. One team designed the brochures, one made the products, and one created the packaging. This experience allowed Stan to grow and demonstrate his leadership and entrepreneurial skills through a naturalistic setting motivated by his interests.

Over the course of the next year, Stan stepped up even more when the horticulture club was tasked with caring for the campus chickens. Stan suggested that the horticulture club form a subgroup called the Chicken Club (to which, of course, he was elected president). As Stan began to take on major responsibilities in the group, he became increasingly worried over who would care for the chickens during summer. How could the group ensure the well-being of the chickens when everyone was on vacation? To make sure the chickens were well kept without his oversight, Stan decided to write a manual entitled Chicken Care. His motivation for the -product allowed him to push past his reluctance to write and overcome his difficulty with spelling and grammar. With assistance from his teacher, he was able to get his ideas on paper. He spent hours poring over the work to make sure that his words were spelled correctly and his ideas were conveyed clearly. His hard work paid off, and the chickens were well taken care of while the Chicken Club was absent.

In the following year, he convinced the head of his school to allow the group to purchase more chickens so that they could start a new business venture—selling eggs! To convince the school of the validity of his idea, he wrote a persuasive business plan complete with numbers and profit estimates. When working with an area of interest, Stan was convincing, organized, and focused. The skills and confidence he gained through this experience were learned in an extracurricular activity and generalized as his work within the classroom began to improve.

Conclusion

So you might be wondering, where is Stan now? Stan is a college graduate, having completed his BA in just three years. Currently, he is working as a grant writer for projects that work to protect the environment. When we look back, who among us could have predicted this outcome from his early trajectory? His teachers worked hard to plant seeds through strength-based, talent-focused education. As we have discussed, this approach offers great promise as we begin to address the complex needs of 2e students. Research, teacher reports, and student growth all provide evidence for the benefit of focusing on what students *can do* instead of what they *can't do*. Contrary to the popular belief that a student's deficits must be remediated before attention can be given to their strengths and interests, we advocate for a strength-based, talent-focused approach in which a student can achieve and find satisfaction in learning.

In this chapter, we introduced ways to become familiar with 2e students and use their strengths so they can contribute and learn in the classroom. We also provided a general overview of what 2e students look like and how we can support them across the school. In the following chapters, these concepts will be extended through the Schoolwide Enrichment Model, which is a standard that has demonstrably improved student achievement, well-being, and productivity in educational systems around the world.

References

Armstrong, M. (2010). *Armstrong's Essential Human Resource Management Practice: A Guide to People Management*. Kogan Page Publishers.

Assouline, S. G., Foley-Nicpon, M., and Dockery, L. (2012). Predicting the academic achievement of gifted students with autism spectrum disorder. *Journal of Autism and Developmental Disorders*, 42(9), 1781–1789. https://doi.org/10.1007/s10803-011-1403-x

Baum, S., Cooper, C. R., and Neu, T. W. (2001). Dual differentiation: An approach for meeting the curricular needs of gifted students with learning disabilities. *Psychology in the Schools*, 38(5), 477–490. https://doi.org/10.1002/pits.1036

Baum, S., Emerick, L. J., Herman, G. N., and Dixon, J. (1989). Identification, programs, and enrichment strategies for gifted learning-disabled youth. *Roeper Review*, 12(1), 48–53. https://doi.org/10.1080/02783198909553230

Baum, S., and Novak, C. (2010). Why isn't talent development on the IEP? SEM and the twice-exceptional learner. *Gifted Education International*, 26(2–3), 249–260. https://doi.org/10.1177/026142941002600311

Baum, S., Schader, R., and Owen, S. (2017). To be gifted and learning disabled: Strength-based strategies for helping twice exceptional students with LD, ADHD, ASD, and more. Prufrock Press

Baum, S., & Schader, R. (2023). Bridges strength-based, talent-focused teaching: Solutions for complex learners. Presentation, Study with the Masters Bridges Graduate School (June 24–29).

Baum, S., and Schader, R. (2024). *Bridges Education Group Toolkit*. Bridges Education Group. https://bridgeseducationgroup.com/

Baum, S., Schader, R. M., and Hébert, T. P. (2014). Through a different lens: Reflecting on a strengths-based, talent-focused approach for 2e learners. *Gifted Child Quarterly*, 58(4), 311–327. https://doi.org/10.1177/0016986214547632

Cleveland Clinic. (2022). *Neurodivergent*. https://my.clevelandclinic.org/health/symptoms/23154-neurodivergent

Dodson, W. (2023, December 20). *New Insights into Rejection-sensitive Dysphoria?* ADDitude. www.additudemag.com/rejection-sensitive-dysphoria-adhd-emotional-dysregulation/

Foley-Nicpon, M., Allmon, A., Sieck, B., and Stinson, R. D. (2011). Empirical investigation of twice-exceptionality: Where have we been and where are we going? *Gifted Child Quarterly*, 55(1), 3–17. https://doi.org/10.1177/0016986210382575

Hansford, S., Whitmore, J., Kraynak, A., and Wingenbach, N. (1987). *Intellectually Gifted Learning Disabled Students: A Special Study*. Council for Exceptional Children.

High School: Robotics Team (2024). *Bridges Academy Biweekly Newsletter*. March 13.

Luscher, B., Mahendra, R., Baum, S., & Schader, R. (2021). *Dual differentiation*. Bridges Education Group.

Reis, S. M., Gelbar, N. W., and Madaus, J. W. (2021). Understanding the academic success of academically talented college students with autism spectrum disorders. *Journal of Autism and Developmental Disorders*. https://doi.org/10.1007/s10803-021-05290-4

Reis, S. M., Gentry, M., and Maxfield, L. R. (1998). The application of enrichment clusters to teachers' classroom practices. *Journal for the Education of the Gifted*, *21*(3), 310–334. https://doi.org/10.1177/016235329802100304

Reis, S. M., Madaus, J. W., Gelbar, N. W., and Miller, L. J. (2022). Strength-based strategies for 2e high school students with autism spectrum disorder. *TEACHING Exceptional Children*, 21(3) 310–334. https://doi.org/10.1177/016235329802100304

Renzulli, J. S. (1978). What makes giftedness? Reexamining a definition. *Phi Delta Kappan*, 60(3), 180–184, 261. www.jstor.org/stable/20299281

Renzulli, J. S., and Reis, S. M. (2014). *The Schoolwide Enrichment Model: A How-to Guide for Educational Excellence* (3rd ed.). Prufrock Press.

Schader, R. M., and Baum, S. M. (2015). *Viewer's Guide for 2e: Twice Exceptional Documentary* [Movie by Thomas Ropelewski]. Studio City, CA: Bridges Academy.

Seligman, M. E. (1999). *Speech at Lincoln Summit—Closing address at the First Positive Psychology Summit held at the Gallup International Research and Education Center in Lincoln, NE, 9–12 September* [Transcript]. Positive Psychology Centre Conference Archives.

Seligman, M. E., and Csikszentmihalyi, M. (2000). *Positive Psychology: An Introduction*. American Psychological Association.

Silberman, S. (2015). *Neurotribes: The Legacy of Autism and the Future of Neurodiversity*. Penguin.

Silverman, L. K. (1989). Invisible gifts, invisible handicaps. *Roeper Review*, 12(1), 37–42. https://doi.org/10.1080/02783198909553228

Sin, N. L., and Lyubomirsky, S. (2009). Enhancing well-being and alleviating depressive symptoms with positive psychology interventions: A practice-friendly meta-analysis. *Journal of Clinical Psychology*, 65(5), 467–487. https://doi.org/10.1002/jclp.20593

2

Using Strength-Based Learning to Promote Socioemotional Well-being and Success

Challenges Faced and Strategies That Work

If you have a 2e student in your class, you are likely aware of how their emotions and behaviors can vary from day to day. At times, your 2e student (or students) can be extremely articulate, informed, and engaged in learning activities. At other times, they may be unpredictable and display behaviors that are not conducive to learning. When 2e students become moody, disengaged, or angry, they may lash out at their support system, including their teachers, counselors, and parents. They might underachieve or fail to produce academic work that matches their potential. You could find that they occasionally refuse to comply with reasonable academic requests and, upon speaking with parents, discover that these behaviors are consistent between school and home. Although these behaviors may seem surprising given the positive students you often see, it is common for 2e students to display seemingly contradictory behaviors. Unfortunately, many 2e students develop problematic behaviors because of challenges or traumas they have faced (Bachtel and Fell, 2022). For example, some students who are 2e display aggressive behavior

DOI: 10.4324/9781003511861-2

that is difficult for teachers to manage as they work diligently to provide students with high-quality learning experiences. Other students who are 2e might misinterpret communication signals, such as eye contact or body language, and struggle to cope with sudden changes in the classroom. This misunderstanding may lead to expressive behaviors that disrupt the classroom.

These behaviors could occur due to a lack of proper support. Some teachers have skewed, negative, or outdated beliefs about smart students with disabilities. For example, one of our colleagues who is a teacher with a son who is 2eASD said that she never believed her son could be autistic because he was so verbal and bright. In her decade of teaching, she argued, she had never encountered an academically talented student with autism. Too often, these types of false assumptions or stereotypes guide teachers' and parents' perceptions, which, in turn, can lead to the under-identification of 2e students.

For a real-world example of a talented individual with autism, consider Temple Grandin, who is one of the most famous neurodiverse individuals in the United States. She is a researcher, scholar, and teacher who has spent her life advocating for a kinder and more humane way to treat livestock used for food. Temple was diagnosed with autism as a child and subsequently became one of the leading voices for autism acceptance worldwide. She has written several books about her experiences growing up, providing an in-depth understanding of the social and emotional challenges of being 2e.

If you want to explore the experiences of being 2e with your students, we recommend reading *Temple Grandin: How the Girl Who Loved Cows Embraced Autism and Changed the World*, a children's book about her life. This might be a good title to use with elementary and secondary students, as it describes the challenges Temple experienced with an overloaded sensory system. The following excerpt is particularly descriptive of the sensory challenges she experienced:

> Like most people with autism, Temple's mind was assaulted by a sensory system that didn't work properly. Her ears and eyes and nose worked fine, but the

information they carried to her brain came through, distorted. Sounds were too loud, scents too strong, words garbled. Sometimes a bright light or a whirring fan was physically painful. She loved flapping flags, but the sight of one was so engrossing, it made it difficult to concentrate on anything else.

To escape the painful noises, confusing words, and overwhelming sensations, Temple would twirl. Many kids like to twirl in circles, but Temple twirled for hours on end. She would also spin coins and jar lids and watch them for hours. Retreating into her own world, she could screen out the confusion around her.

(p. 2)

Despite encountering numerous challenges associated with navigating a neurotypical society as an individual with autism, Temple's narrative is one of triumph. She achieved success and garnered widespread respect as an academic expert in the fields of animal science and welfare. By leveraging her personal experiences, she conducted global outreach efforts aimed at raising awareness about the far-reaching impacts of autism. Temple used her experiences to travel the world and educate others about the impacts of autism. She stands as a powerful advocate for individuals on the autism spectrum, as she showcases the innate potential that lies within 2e individuals.

Now, let's examine the experiences of a 2e student in the classroom. The case studies of Jade and Luis below provide very different scenarios of 2e students who are underachieving in school.

Jade

Despite experiencing learning problems in school for several years, Jade was a student who was identified as 2e when she was a seventh-grade student. As she grew older, her skill gaps became more apparent as her textbooks grew more challenging. In sixth grade, her parents noted a sudden decline in her grades. Her teacher and the reading specialist referred her for assessment when they noticed a significant discrepancy between her verbal, reading, and writing skills. A battery of tests indicated an IQ score of 129; however, the assessor found a large discrepancy between Jade's performance areas. Jade was identified as having poor decoding skills, with independent reading below the second-grade level. Further assessment with a school psychologist found that she was a very capable student with significant disabilities in reading, information processing, and auditory processing. She was also identified as having ADHD. Despite her identification, her grades continued to slip, and her reading failed to improve and progress over the next few years. She was increasingly labeled an underachiever and her teachers described her as a 'bright but unmotivated' student. During her adolescence, Jade became anxious, depressed, and discouraged as she continued to struggle in school. Over the course of her academic career, school turned into a place of anxiety for Jade.

Luis

Luis was an academically talented fifth-grade boy who had been previously diagnosed with inattentive ADHD. His disability manifested in slow processing skills and weak executive function skills, which made it challenging for him to plan, organize, and follow through with almost all academic tasks, especially his work in school. When in class, he read slowly and took time to answer questions, respond to requests, and complete work. Luis was unable to follow directions, consistently missed deadlines, and forgot to turn in assignments. Outside of school, his home life was exhausting, as his parents were constantly pushing him to complete schoolwork at home. This caused problems, resulting in fights and arguments about going to school. Luis began falling further behind every year.

Understanding the Social and Emotional Needs of Students Who Are 2e

As you can see from the examples above, the diversity of these students provides a significant challenge as we work to support them in the classroom. In some tasks, some 2e students work at average or above-average levels of productivity. For example, a student identified as 2e with dyslexia may excel during a verbal discussion about a complex topic. However, this same student might fail when working on any assignment that requires independent reading or writing. Other 2e students might fail to meet deadlines, complete work, or demonstrate consistent study habits. Others still cannot plan for a simple project that should be achievable.

The differing personal profiles of these students make it even more challenging to support them. For example, some students identified as 2e are talented in communication, while others cannot communicate at all. These types of dissimilarities often mean that students feel awkward and out of place in school. Imagine what it must feel like to truly understand something in a deep and complex way but not be able to explain your answer to others. School can be stressful and scary for students who are 2e and those who cannot read well are often terrified that they will be called on to read aloud, while those who cannot write are often apprehensive about every written assignment.

The final layer of complication in understanding these students lies in their self-concept. They often believe that they are smart enough to be able to handle any challenge without support, even if it lies in an area related to their disability. This can lead to intense frustration as students are forced to confront their deficits. Teachers and parents often struggle to understand how much and what types of help to give to 2e students. They might ask for support one day while acting upset when a caring adult offers to help the next. Teachers and parents of these students often struggle to understand how much to help and assist these young people.

The Hierarchy of Needs

To help us figure out what support is right and under what circumstances, we can turn to Maslow's hierarchy of needs. According to Maslow (1954), human needs are arranged in a specific order, with physiological (survival) needs at the bottom and creative and intellectually oriented 'self-actualization' needs at the top. Maslow's hierarchy of needs is a theory that we should consider when we discuss the social and emotional experiences of these students. Maslow's five-tier model of human needs is often drawn as a pyramid, with the five levels described as physiological, safety, love/belonging, esteem, and self-actualization. Students' first level of needs (food, safety) must be met before we can consider higher needs. Establishing physiological well-being might involve providing these students with a snack or bathroom break. Creating a safe environment may entail addressing potential stressors such as buzzing lighting, crowded areas, and excessive classroom activity.

When we think about psychological and esteem needs, take a moment to consider what it would be like to know the answers but not be able to communicate them to your teachers. Academic frustrations abound for this group, as do feelings of being different, incompetent, and afraid to be viewed as lacking. Feelings of anxiety can become the norm for these students, which can contribute to low self-esteem. Students identified with 2e may have been initially happy and engaged in primary grades but begin to fall behind as they get older. Some beg their parents to let them stay home—especially if home has always been a *safe* place. For students who appeared academically inclined and happy when they were younger, this shift can be extremely detrimental and have a profound impact on their self-esteem. Remember that the disabilities of these students often manifest in lower achievement and inability to achieve goals they view as attainable. When they are not identified as talented, they are solely recognized for their disabilities and subsequently struggle to complete tasks that classroom teachers would reasonably expect them to finish. In order to support the psychological well-being of 2e students, we must view them from a perspective of strength.

Support Beyond the Hierarchy of Needs

In addition to ensuring that the needs of these students are met, teachers should be aware that students who are 2e experience asynchronous development. Asynchronous development in academically talented students occurs when their various areas of development grow at different rates. This happens unevenly which differs from their same-aged peers. For example, a student who reads six or seven years above grade level could still have a meltdown in a grocery store if her parents do not buy her the type of ice cream she wants. Outstanding intellectual ability in 2e students often means that students' strengths exceed both their same-aged peers and their own physiological development. This type of development may be accompanied by heightened sensitivity that some scholars in the field believe can lead to complex experiences for talented students. Common reactions to asynchronous development in 2e students can result in students feeling overwhelmed and lead to outbursts, frustrations, and a lack of empathy for others as they are overwhelmed by their own challenges.

To support these students, it is helpful to begin by providing a classroom that is secure (Porges, 2022; Reis, Gelbar, and Madaus, 2021, 2022). In this chapter, we dive deeper into some social and emotional challenges faced by this group and discuss strategies to help them modulate their emotions. Your support and compassion can lead to feelings of safety, both in school and at home. We also suggest ways in which teachers and parents can help these students to emerge as emotionally well-regulated and socially confident. Though achieving this goal may take some time, your efforts will prove invaluable to the social and emotional well-being of your 2e students!

Social and Emotional Challenges

You may have found in your own teaching experience that it is difficult, if not impossible, to grow and support students' academic skills without addressing their social and emotional challenges. As noted, 2e students often struggle to reach their full potential as their specific needs overshadow their strengths. Many of these students require special education services for academic, behavioral, and social-emotional support. As a growing body of research has contributed to our understanding of the special needs of these students, one thing is clear—many talented students with disabilities are recognized first and foremost for their deficits.

Many 2e students struggle to regulate their emotions when they encounter direct requests from teachers who expect that they can easily complete tasks. For example, activities like circle time can be challenging for students who find it difficult to stay still, especially when these events are scheduled for the start of the school day. For some 2e students with ADHD or ASD, beginning the day without the opportunity to move around sets them up for failure, as they have difficulty transitioning from home to school. Another hidden stressor relates to asking these students to show their work, as they may struggle to explain their answers. Emotional responses in these scenarios are typically exacerbated as many 2e students have difficulty with eye contact and direct communication. Daily stressors like these can lead to students shutting down, as they constantly feel anxious, defeated, and overwhelmed.

These problems often manifest in social-emotional disturbances outside of the classroom. When discussing their 2e children, many parents describe children who beg not to go to school, become blank when reflecting on their day, or have intense outbursts as soon as they get in the door. One parent that we worked with told us a story about picking up her daughter from her large high school that her daughter hated. The mom described looking out over the school yard and seeing large, happy groups of students chatting with each other, walking out of class with smiles. In contrast, her daughter slunk from behind a large concrete column to walk to the car, appearing sad, alone, and isolated. That moment, the mom explained, was the instant she knew something had to change.

The deficit model creates or worsens many of these social-emotional problems. Your 2e students may not even recognize that they have talents due to the learning and socioemotional challenges that they face. This leads to low feelings of self-efficacy and self-esteem. However, with the right types of support and encouragement, students of all abilities can achieve at high levels and regulate their behaviors.

Academic Challenges

You may have been under the impression that, as a group, neurotypical gifted students are not as well-adjusted as their peers.

Researchers in gifted education have found that high-ability students are generally as adjusted as others who are identified as academically talented (Neihart et al., 2002). An exception to these findings is students with 2e. The combination of high potential and learning difficulties poses numerous social and emotional challenges for these learners (Reis, Baum, and Burke, 2014).

As we have noted, one of the most pervasive problems affecting this population is underperformance, which may further contribute to educators' tendency to overlook students' abilities and fail to refer them for assessment. Some teachers hold outdated beliefs about high-potential students with disabilities and may not see their positive characteristics in light of their challenges. This often keeps 2e students from receiving proper talent development. In 1985, Whitmore and Maker summarized their analysis of this problem as below, and unfortunately, some of their statements continue to hold true today.

> Intellectually gifted individuals with specific learning disabilities are the most misjudged, misunderstood, and neglected segment of the student population and the community. Teachers, counselors, and others are inclined to overlook signs of intellectual giftedness and to focus attention on such deficits as poor spelling, reading, and writing. Expectations for academic achievement generally are inaccurate—either too high and unrealistically positive or too low and discouraging of high aspirations. It is not uncommon for students identified as 2e to be told that college study is inappropriate for them, that professional careers will be unattainable, and that jobs requiring only mechanical or physical abilities are more fitting to their abilities. Without equal opportunity to try, these individuals may be denied access to appropriate educational and professional career opportunities.
>
> (pp. 204–205)

There is good news, however. Our more recent research has found that classroom and content area teachers are beginning to recognize the potential inherent in this population. This has led to an increased willingness to provide enrichment for this group (Reis et al., 2021; 2022). This shift may have been positively influenced by educational research regarding 2e students and updated theories of intelligence and giftedness (Gardner and Wolf, 1983; Renzulli and Reis, 1977; Sternberg et al., 1981). These theories suggest that the potential of some students may not be accurately captured by previous measures of intelligence, which tended to view giftedness as synonymous with good behavior and scores on an intelligence test.

The notion that 2e students are gifted has been validated by years of study. As early as 1937, Samuel Orton (1989) found wide ranges of intelligence among non-readers with specific reading and writing disabilities. At the time, he argued that this was indicative of learning problems in many high-ability students, which has since been corroborated by modern literature (Maddocks, 2020). When students experience learning problems, they often experience feelings of inferiority, an inability to persevere in the accomplishment of goals, and a general lack of self-confidence. Another recent study that explored the academic self-efficacy of 2e students (Wang and Neihart, 2015) found that high self-efficacy scores can be influenced by parents, teachers, peers, and previously attained achievement. These conclusions highlight the incredible importance of cultivating positive expectations and providing strength-based support to 2e students.

As we have stated, your smart students with disabilities may find it challenging to understand why they know an answer but struggle to communicate their ideas effectively. Each day, they face the conflicting realities of high potentiality and learning difficulties. This dichotomy may, in turn, create social and emotional difficulties, as students often lack the tools to navigate this confusing experience. A previous study by Reis, Neu, and McGuire (1997) examined academically successful college students who are 2e. All participants recalled negative, and in many cases painful, memories from their elementary and secondary school years. These negative school experiences were frequently linked directly to their disabilities and included repeated punishment for not completing work on time, grade retention, placement in inappropriate special education classrooms, and poor treatment by peers and teachers. Multiple participants reported being labeled as 'lazy' and were told that they needed to 'shape up' and 'work harder.'

Despite being enrolled in competitive universities, these talented students carried traumatic memories from their earlier educational experiences. When we reflect on these students' experiences, we can consider the impact their teachers had on their sense of self-efficacy. It is likely that most teachers recognized these students' brightness and superior skills, which were not reflected in their writing and reading scores. Confused by the discrepancy between potential and achievement, teachers may have assumed the students were lazy. This misconception likely deprived the students of the necessary tools and strategies to build academic success.

As educators, we know that students should receive attention for their academic needs and not for the negative traits commonly ascribed to them. For example, high-potential students with ADHD may demonstrate behaviors such as inattention, high energy level, and impulsivity. These students may experience inattention when they are not appropriately challenged, but they may also demonstrate a high energy and strong commitment to excel in areas of intense interest. Many high-potential students like these tire easily of repetitive and unchallenging activities but can sustain focused attention when they are working on stimulating tasks that they enjoy doing. This can have a direct and detrimental impact on their mental health.

Our colleague Terry Neu (1994) studied 2e students and identified various issues that characterize their experiences. In one case, a highly gifted girl with an undiagnosed learning disability and chronic underachievement received no support or help in school. It wasn't until she attempted suicide in ninth grade that she was referred to a psychologist and psychiatrist. A neuropsychological assessment revealed that she suffered from both a learning disability and bipolar disorder. Under the care of a mental health team, her treatment progressed and her academic performance improved. Educators must be aware of signs of psychological distress in students with both talents and disabilities. It is crucial to refer students who may be experiencing psychological problems to the school counselor or school psychologist.

Supporting 2e Students

The more strategies teachers have to address the needs of 2e students, the easier it will be to effectively reach and teach them. As you know, different students require different approaches. Educators are more likely to succeed with 2e students when they help them to develop self-control and self-empowerment, which in turn increases their desire to succeed and meet personal goals. When teachers implement strategies that enable them to both identify and develop individual gifts and talents, 2e students begin to improve their social, emotional, and academic regulation. Applying a strengths-based approach to teaching 2e students focuses on their unique abilities, enabling them to become more engaged, productive, and resilient. By shifting your perspective from remediating weaknesses to developing gifts and talents, your students will reap significant rewards.

You may be wondering about the most effective ways to support these students. We recommend individually selected interest-based enrichment activities, described in subsequent chapters, as a productive and creative way to engage this population. These opportunities have been shown to enhance self-esteem and reduce frustration. When students have mentors that help them focus on their interests and talents, they perceive school as a place to help them grow as individuals. In other words, if you enable your students to explore what they are interested in, you watch them grow!

Further, when educators encourage students to view their identified disabilities as personal strengths, they create an environment where students can develop resilience, confidence, and a growth mindset. As students learn to overcome their challenges through compensatory strategies, they can improve their individual persistence, develop their talents, and strengthen their self-control. When that happens, students who are 2e will have more opportunities to be successful. In short, we advise teachers to use their students' strengths to develop areas that need improvement. This approach not only helps students embrace their unique abilities but promotes inclusivity and understanding among peers, which can lead to a more supportive and empowering school environment.

To summarize, students identified as 2e comprise a unique population who are at high risk for social/emotional issues. These issues can result in unresolved social and emotional problems that diminish the full development of talent in gifted students, resulting in the underachievement of many talented young people. Even if you are motivated enough to seek guidance from this book, you may sometimes struggle with how to support your 2e students. When in doubt, teachers can reach out to school counselors and mental health professionals for help with their disabled students. The incorporation of group and individual counseling, as well as tailored emotional programs, can address the unique challenges faced by 2e students. These approaches improve academic performance while offering opportunities for students to learn effective coping mechanisms, express emotions, and manage heightened sensitivities. Working with a school-based mental health professional, either individually or with groups of students, encourages students to develop positive peer relationships. The increased social and emotional support from these positive relationships will go a long way in addressing students' low academic achievement.

Increasing Self-Regulation in Students Identified as 2e

In this section, we will explore self-regulation, which is an area that many students with 2e identify as critically important in their academic lives and emotional well-being. Our research about self-regulation suggests that some smart students with disabilities possess more self-regulated learning strategies than their peers. These strategies have been learned over time as students use them to survive and cope within neurotypical society. Unfortunately, some social conditions or personal challenges may prevent students from developing self-regulated learning strategies. Some students with high potential find it difficult to learn self-regulation when it is not taught, modeled, or rewarded by adults. Even if 2e students regularly interact with adults who demonstrate self-regulatory abilities, they may struggle to learn and apply these skills themselves. This can be due to peer pressure or a reluctance to adopt the strategies used by their parents or teachers in their home or school environments.

The Process of Building Self-Regulation

Self-regulation is an integrated learning process where individuals engage in constructive behaviors that facilitate learning. These self-regulated behaviors include making helpful, constructive choices that positively impact students' learning success. When students self-regulate, they learn to plan and adapt strategies to achieve their goals as their learning environments change.

According to Zimmerman (1989), self-regulated learning involves the regulation of three general zones:

1. **Self-regulation of behavior** refers to the ability of individuals to actively manage and control their actions and resources in a way that supports their learning and goal achievement. It involves the ability to manage time, seek help, and select an appropriate study environment.
2. **Self-regulation of motivation and affect** refers to the ability of individuals to control and modify their motivational beliefs and emotional responses to enhance learning and goal achievement. This involves self-efficacy, goal orientation, and emotional regulation.
3. **Self-regulation of cognition** refers to the ability of individuals to manage and apply cognitive strategies effectively to enhance their learning processes. This involves the use of cognitive strategies, metacognition, and self-reflection.

Many gifted students lack self-regulation. Helping them acquire specific strategies enables them to gain better control over their behavior, which supports their efforts to decrease negative choices and increase positive ones. The quality and variety of these self-regulation processes are crucial. You will quickly learn that no single self-regulation strategy works for all students, and using only a few strategies will not be equally effective for the same person across tasks or settings. It is important to help students learn to use various skills rather than one single strategy. By doing so, we remind students that both their goals and their use of self-regulation strategies will grow and broaden over time. Teachers should work with students to help them persist through challenges, which is especially critical for talented students with difficulties in emotion regulation. Consider our next case study as we explore skills for developing self-regulation.

Maia

Maia, an eighth-grade student, was identified as gifted in first grade. Throughout her time in school she struggled with attention and was subsequently classified with ADHD. She read at the seventh-grade level by the time she finished second grade and always scored at 99% on standardized achievement tests. She excelled in language arts and had high scores in math, science, and writing. Maia did not like math but coasted through the curriculum between first and seventh grade, all while doing minimal homework and receiving top grades. Because of her scores on achievement tests and her previous grades, she was recommended for an advanced algebra class in eighth grade. For the first time, she encountered real academic challenge. She began to struggle in class and told her parents that she was 'not that smart.' As she began to doubt her abilities, her confidence dropped, and she quit whenever she encountered a math homework problem she could not immediately solve. Maia's parents encouraged her to keep trying on her homework, but she would tell them she would ask her teacher for help the next day. Main found that the answers to problems were in the back of her math book, and after a minute of trying, she would look them up. Maia's actions dissuaded her from learning how to tackle and manage challenges. She failed tests, became convinced she was terrible at math, and told her parents that she wanted to drop out of the algebra class. How can Maia, a smart student who struggles with focus and attention, gain the self-regulation skills she needs to persist in the face of challenge?

Phases of Self-Regulation

Most studies have shown that there are three cyclical phases that occur when students begin to learn self-regulation skills.

Forethought/Pre-action is the phase that comes before the actual work starts. During this phase, students can be asked to write down the task. This helps to reduce anxiety as it minimizes the unknown and develops an understanding of the activity. It sets realistic expectations, which makes the task more approachable and appealing. Students can then set goals related to the activity. These should have specific outcomes and be arranged

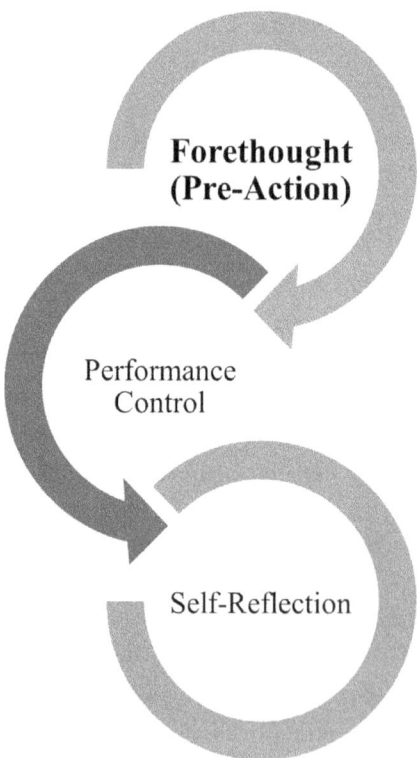

FIGURE 2.1 Phase 1: Forethought/Pre-Action

from short- to long-term. During this phase, you should ask your student to consider:

- When will you start?
- Where will you work?
- How will you get started?
- Are there any obstacles that might stop you?
- How about supports that could help you?

During this step, students like Maia should be encouraged to think about their homework and reflect on any barriers to completion. Is there a better time or place to do her homework? Should she start in school with her friends? Can she plan to spend at least five minutes on a problem before giving up and moving on? Can she find a study buddy for after school? Should she ask her teacher or parents to find a tutor? By answering these questions, Maia may be empowered to reduce her anxiety by creating her own solutions.

In this phase, students should ask themselves to consider what works best for them during their learning task. In other words, what processes help them to learn? By understanding their thoughts, students can maintain their motivation during a task. Additionally, this process helps students to identify their own areas of strength. During this phase, you should ask your student to consider:

- Have you accomplished this task in the past? If yes, how so?
- What distractions have you encountered?
- Are your assignments taking more time than you thought?
- What helps you to accomplish the most?
- When your work gets hard, what can you say to motivate yourself? Is there a phrase, affirmation, or quote that you like?

Students like Maia should consider why math (and not other content areas) is getting harder. When she gets angry and

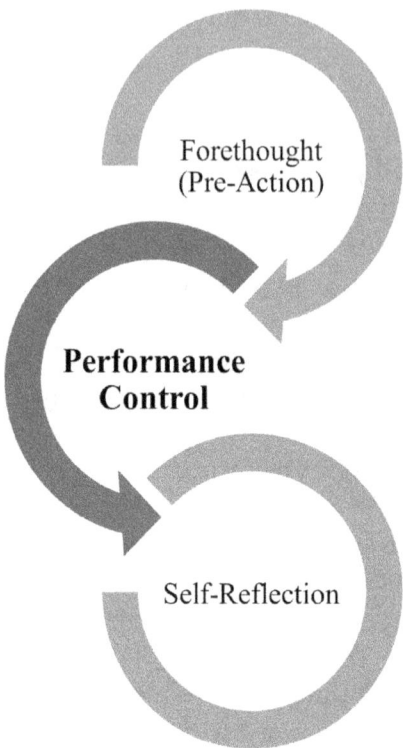

FIGURE 2.2 Phase 2: Performance Control

frustrated, what can she do? Should she stop and take a break? Should she do her math homework first rather than putting it off until later? Should she have background music or work in silence? She is supposed to be using and considering what has worked best for her—what is her success or failure with some of the strategies she has mentioned? Is there anything new Maia can try?

The development of good self-regulation typically involves the following tasks:

a. Self-observation—ask students to think about what they are doing in a challenging learning task. Have them keep notes/records of what they will try.
b. Self-analysis—ask students to consider what has worked and compare their performance to their predetermined

goal (e.g., re-examining answers; checking what you do and what works).

c. Self-reaction—ask students to consider their own personal processes and what it felt like to succeed at something. This might include previously attained goals, plans, or outcomes. Have them self-administer praise or criticism; rehearse proximal goal-setting; restructure their environment, or ask for help.

Table 2.1 Self-Regulation Strategies

What are the individual self-regulation strategies that are usually used by successful students? They usually involve personal, behavioral, and environmental strategies.
A. **Personal:** These strategies usually involve how a student organizes and interprets information and can include: 1. **Organizing and transforming information** • outlining • summarizing • rearrangement of materials • highlighting • flashcards/index cards • draw pictures, diagrams, charts • webs/mapping 2. **Goal setting and planning/standard setting** • sequencing, timing, completing • time management and pacing 3. **Keeping records and monitoring** • note-taking • lists of errors made • record of marks • portfolio, keeping all drafts of assignments 4. **Rehearsing and memorizing** (written or verbal; overt or covert) • mnemonic devices • teaching someone else the material • making sample questions

(Continued)

Table 2.1 (Continued)

> - using mental imagery
> - using repetition
> B. **Behavioral:** These strategies involve actions that the student takes.
>   1. **Self-evaluating** (checking quality or progress)
>   - task analysis (What does the teacher want me to do? What do I want out of it?)
>   - self-instructions; enactive feedback
>   - attentiveness
>   - task analysis (What does the teacher want me to do? What do I want out of it?)
>   2. **Self-consequating**
>   - treats to motivate; self-reinforcement
>   - arrangement or imagination of punishments; delay of gratification
> C. **Environmental:** These strategies involve seeking assistance and structuring of the physical study environment.
>   1. **Seeking information** (library, Internet)
>   - library resources
>   - Internet resources
>   - reviewing cards
>   - rereading records, tests, textbooks
>   2. **Environmental structuring**
>   - selecting or arranging the physical setting
>   - isolating/eliminating or minimizing distractions
>   - break up study periods and spread them over time
>   3. **Seeking social assistance**
>   - from peers
>   - from teachers or other adults
>   - emulate exemplary models

As you have seen, understanding how executive functions, self-regulation, and metacognition can contribute to student success is essential for healthy social and emotional growth. 2e students often need guidance in understanding their strengths and weaknesses to learn how to use self-regulation strategies effectively. To support them, you can work with your students to develop personal plans designed to increase their self-regulation skills. We have included a sample plan in Appendix A. Typically, these outlines help students improve their metacognition. Metacognition involves using self-knowledge to understand a learning task or situation and identify appropriate steps and responses. Students who practice metacognition can enhance their ability to sustain action and attention while planning, organizing, and developing strategies. Metacognitive strategies train students to think about their thinking and engage in the self-reflection and questioning practices that are particularly important for success.

What Else Can Teachers Do to Help?

As we discussed in Chapter 1, too many educational efforts are aimed at 'fixing' our students. Many students with 2e have emotional challenges that include feeling different, experiencing anxiety and depression, and becoming socially isolated. As these challenges begin to grow, 2e students often become unproductive, disruptive, and anxious about school, all while lacking motivation to achieve. 2e students need to achieve belonging, autonomy, and competence in order to succeed. As such, they need to feel that they belong in school and have a physical environment in which they can be successful. They desire choice and flexibility of instruction and benefit greatly from strength-based learning in their classrooms. The example in Chapter 1 outlines the environmental conditions in the following five areas that encourage and support successful learning:

- **The physical environment** must create conditions that enable students to regulate their physical needs.
- As discussed in later chapters, **the academic/intellectual environment** must provide options for interest and strength-based learning.
- **The social environment** must give opportunities for students to spend time with students who share their interests.

- **The emotional environment** must enable students to feel psychologically safe.
- **The creative environment** must give students a place for ideas, creative products, and brainstorming to emerge.

Several specific strategies for helping students are discussed below. They range from affirming talents to providing opportunities for students to develop interests and interact with advanced content.

Identify Talents and Strengths

In our research, the confidence of 2e students increased when their teachers reminded them they had both academic talent and high potential. Several explained that when they learned they had some academic talent, they began to actually believe they could be successful in school. They argued that support from teachers and parents to develop their talents was crucial for their success. Through our research, we also learned something else. Despite being identified as gifted, several students were not allowed to participate in advanced academic opportunities. Although their teachers and counselors told them that the advanced classes would be too stressful, current evidence indicates that classes and content that were too easy had a higher impact on anxiety in 2e students. This had a negative impact on students who felt simultaneously bored and underwhelmed. As teachers, you can combat this by supporting students in their areas of interest. If you do that, you can change a student's life!

Provide Enrichment and Strength-Based Learning Experiences with Opportunities for Creative Expression

As we have suggested in the previous chapter, strength-based learning experiences can make a profound difference in the academic lives of 2e students (don't worry, we will explain how this is done in subsequent chapters). In our research involving 2eASD students, we found that nearly three-quarters of participants were enrolled in advanced, honors, or college credit-bearing courses in their areas of strength and interest while in high school. Almost all the students we studied were involved in at least one interest-based extracurricular activity. These activities were exceedingly important for students to pursue their interests and develop their strengths. Additionally, opportunities like these can help students gain leadership experience and find academic peers with similar interests. About half of the successful students we studied also participated in residential camp/program experiences in areas of interest, such as debate, weather, theater, and the arts. These students reported that these programs helped them concentrate on their strengths and interests while learning to communicate and build friendships with others involved who share these interests.

Environmental Changes in the Classroom or Home: Providing a Psychologically Safe Environment

Whether students are at home or in their classroom, it is essential for them to have a place where they feel safe. Many successful 2e students have described having a designated safe space in school, such as a guidance counselor's office, a desk in the back of a room, and a bench in a quiet hallway. Many 2e students struggle with overstimulation and exhaustion related to on-going social and academic stress. These designated areas often provide them with a moment of rest and respite, allowing them to reengage with learning later on. Notably, we have never heard of a 2e student who felt comfortable or safe when assigned a spot right in front of the class next to the teacher's chair.

Teach Compensation Strategies

Many 2e students benefit from compensation strategies. These tactics involve methods and techniques that students can use to leverage their strengths and overcome or mitigate their challenges. Several compensation strategies can be used by 2e students to help regulate their social and emotional difficulties and succeed in school. Here are some ideas:

a) Help students develop deliberate study strategies (i.e., retyping or rewriting notes, chunking study time over a few days instead of cramming, mental mapping).
b) Let them use specific cognitive/learning strategies (i.e., having discussions about challenging subjects, teaching difficult concepts to friends, working through advanced problems).
c) Provide various environmental accommodations (i.e., going to the school library to work on something important if the classroom is overstimulating, taking a walk around the building, having a break in a safe space).
d) Counsel in specific areas that address social and emotional challenges (i.e., prosocial behaviors, mindfulness strategies for regulation, self-care).
e) Encourage self-advocacy (i.e., asking a teacher for help in a specific area, setting a boundary with a friend, reporting concerns to the appropriate authority).
f) Create an individual plan incorporating a focus on metacognition and executive functions (more on this in subsequent chapters).

As you can see, providing appropriate programming that enhances strengths, celebrates a diverse range of talents, and emphasizes gifts works best!

Reflecting on Our Case Studies

Why do students like Jade and Luis fail to recognize their own potential? As we discussed, these students have undiagnosed disabilities. They may lack a sense of self-efficacy, goal-directedness, or self-regulation. Others still may underachieve in response to inappropriate educational conditions or environments. For these students, it is often teachers and school staff who make the biggest difference in their attainment. As you learn to recognize your students' unique talents and challenges, you will be able to adjust and modify educational conditions, and undoubtedly, your students will be able to achieve at higher levels.

While it is impossible to specifically define the characteristics of every underachieving student, there are common characteristics that you probably recognize. Some underachieving, high-potential students will later, after years of struggle, be identified as 2e. You know some of these characteristics already and may have a negative perspective on these behaviors. Although this perspective is understandable, with this chapter we encourage you to challenge those beliefs. Instead of focusing on the negative characteristics that are commonly ascribed to underachieving 2e students, we hope to shift the focus to the positive attributes of these talented students. Below, in Figure 2.4, we depict the findings of Frasier and Passow (1994), who noted that these basic attributes of giftedness are similar across exceptionalities.

Your high-potential students likely engage in behaviors that demonstrate one or several of these common characteristics. Students who are identified as 2e may only demonstrate one or two of these attributes, but your increased knowledge of their strengths will help you to challenge prior beliefs. Without a doubt, your students will flourish as a result of an open and positive approach to their unique abilities.

In addition to displaying some of these positive characteristics, students who are 2e may also demonstrate anxiety, intense emotionality, unrealistic expectations of self, a tendency toward intense frustration, disruptive or withdrawn behavior, feelings of learned helplessness, and low self-esteem. A more comprehensive list of characteristics, both positive and negative, is provided in Table 2.3 below.

Table 2.2 Common Attributes of Giftedness

♦ Motivation	♦ Insight
♦ Advanced Interests	♦ Reasoning
♦ Communication Skills	♦ Imagination/Creativity
♦ Problem-Solving Ability	♦ Sense of Humor
♦ Well-developed Memory	♦ Advanced Ability to Understand Symbol Systems
♦ Inquiry	

Table 2.3 Characteristics of 2e Students

Characteristics that Mask High Potential and Result in Underachievement	Characteristics that Demonstrate Strengths and High Potential
◆ Frustration ◆ Learned Helplessness ◆ General Lack of Motivation ◆ Disruptive Classroom Behavior ◆ Perfectionism ◆ Anxiety ◆ Depression ◆ Oversensitivity ◆ Failure to Complete Assignments ◆ Lack of Organizational Skills ◆ Demonstration of Poor Listening and Concentration Skills ◆ Deficiency in Memory and Perceptive Tasks ◆ Low Self-esteem ◆ Unrealistic Self-Expectations ◆ Poor Social Skills	◆ Advanced Vocabulary ◆ Wide Variety of Interests ◆ Strong Focus on Interests ◆ Exceptional Analytic Abilities ◆ High Levels of Creativity ◆ Advanced Problem-Solving Skills ◆ Aptitude for Divergent Ideas and Solutions ◆ Topic-Specific Aptitude (artistic, musical, or mechanical) ◆ Good Memory ◆ Task Commitment ◆ Strong Spatial Abilities

Conclusion

In summary, many students identified as 2e face social, emotional, and learning challenges, and teachers can help students manage and self-regulate these behaviors. By focusing on their interests and talents and providing an environment that is safe and accepts and values individual differences, you can support students as they develop an awareness of their own strengths and weaknesses. It is important to understand that the healthy social and emotional adjustment of students with disabilities matters greatly. Academic offerings that reflect students' interests both in school and in areas outside of traditional academic subjects can help to identify students' strengths and develop their interests. That is just one reason we recommend high-interest enrichment, talent development opportunities, and extracurricular opportunities, in addition to engaging academic experiences, to help develop strengths and increase students' engagement and enjoyment in school.

Over the decades that we have studied and supported 2e students, we have observed their semi-universal strengths. These include areas such as fine attention to detail and empathy with others who also experience challenges. We have seen character strengths that have emerged over time, such as loyalty to their friends and high levels of honesty and integrity. Many students identified as 2e have the ability to focus for hours on end, with strong concentration skills and technical proficiencies. Many excel in memory and in creative thinking, offering unique solutions to problems. Most students identified as 2e have a commitment to honesty, straightforward communication, rule-following, and logical thinking. As we discuss the social and emotional well-being of these students, we cannot forget to honor the strengths that they possess and nurture them to address problems and arrive at unique solutions.

References

Bachtel, K., and Fell, R. (2022). Trauma induced 2eity: Preventing psychological injury of gifted children in the classroom. In F. H. R. Piske, K. H. Collins, and K. B. Arnstein (Eds.). *Critical Issues in Servicing Twice Exceptional Students: Socially, Emotionally, and Culturally Framing Learning Exceptionalities* (pp. 87–105). Springer International Publishing.

Frasier, M. M., and Passow, A. H. (1994). *Toward a New Paradigm for Identifying Talent Potential* (Research Monograph 94112). University of Connecticut, The National Research Center on the Gifted and Talented. https://nrcgt.uconn.edu/wp-content/uploads/sites/953/2015/04/rm94112.pdf

Gardner, H., and Wolf, D. (1983). *Waves and Streams of Symbolization*. In D. R. Rogers and J. A. Sloboda (Eds.), *The Acquisition of Symbolic Skills* (pp. 19–42). Plenum.

Maddocks, D. L. (2020). Cognitive and achievement characteristics of students from a national sample identified as potentially twice exceptional (gifted with a learning disability). *Gifted Child Quarterly*, 64(1), 3–18. https://doi.org/10.1177/0016986219886668

Maslow, A. H. (1954). *Motivation and Personality*. Harpers.

Neihart, M., Reis, S. M., Robinson, N. M., and Moon, S. M. (Eds.). (2002). *The Social and Emotional Development of Gifted Children: What Do We Know?* Prufrock Press.

Neu, T. (1994, Winter). Emotional or behavioral disorders: Classroom conflicts. *The National Research Center on the Gifted and Talented Newsletter*. https://nrcgt.uconn.edu/newsletters/winter945/

Orton, S. T. (1989). *Reading, Writing, and Speech Problems in Children and Selected Papers*. Pro-Ed.

Porges, S. W. (2022). Polyvagal theory: A science of safety. *Frontiers in Integrative Neuroscience*, 16, 1–15. https://doi.org/10.3389/fnint.2022.871227

Reis, S. M., Baum, S. M., and Burke, E. (2014). An operational definition of 2e learners: Implications and applications. *Gifted Child Quarterly*, 58(3), 217–230. https://doi.org/10.1177/0016986214534976

Reis, S. M., Gelbar, N. W., and Madaus, J. W. (2021). Understanding the academic success of academically talented college students with autism spectrum disorders. *Journal of Autism and Developmental Disorders*. https://doi.org/10.1007/s10803-021-05290-4

Reis, S. M., Gentry, M., and Maxfield, L. R. (1998). The application of enrichment clusters to teachers' classroom practices. *Journal for the Education of the Gifted*, 21(3), 310–334. https://doi.org/10.1177/016235329802100304

Reis, S. M., Madaus, J. W., Gelbar, N. W., and Miller, L. J. (2022). Strength-based strategies for 2e high school students with autism spectrum disorder. *TEACHING Exceptional Children*, 21(3), 310–334. https://doi.org/10.1177/016235329802100304

Reis, S. M., Neu, T. W., and McGuire, J. M. (1997). Case studies of high ability students with learning disabilities who have achieved. *Exceptional Children*, 63(4), 1–12.

Renzulli, J. S., and Reis, S. M. (1997). *The Schoolwide Enrichment Model: A Comprehensive Plan for Educational Excellence*. Creative Learning Press.

Sternberg, R. J., Conway, B. E., Ketron, J. L., and Bernstein, M. (1981). People's conceptions of intelligence. *Journal of Personality and Social Psychology*, 41(1), 86–93. https://doi.org/10.1177/001698628102500208

Wang, C. W., and Neihart, M. (2015). Academic self-concept and academic self-efficacy: Self-beliefs enable academic achievement of 2e students. *Roeper Review*, 37(2), 63–73. https://doi.org/10.1080/02783193.2015.1008660

Whitmore, J. R., and Maker, C. J. (1985). *Intellectual Giftedness in Disabled Persons*. Aspen Publishers.

Zimmerman, B. J. (1989). A social cognitive view of self-regulated academic learning. *Journal of Educational Psychology*, 81(3), 329–339. https://psycnet.apa.org/doi/10.1037/0022-0663.81.3.329

3

Identifying Students' Strengths and Interests

Getting Started

As we highlighted with the case study of Stan in Chapter 1, most 2e students love to engage in activities that personally excite them. Similarly, it is a rare teacher who does not enjoy helping students develop their interests and strengths in subjects they love. It is undoubtedly more fulfilling to watch students succeed than to watch them suffer from boredom and loss of engagement, which can occur with the rigid expectations of a typical curriculum. However, many teachers do not know or have not had time to think about how to develop their students' strengths and interests.

Identifying Your Students' Strengths, Talents, and Interests

As you read this chapter, you will gain a better understanding of how to identify your students' strengths, talents, and interests. You will be equipped with tools to aid in identifying your students' preferred ways of learning and the projects they may wish to pursue. We developed these resources to help you create opportunities for your students to pursue interest-based activities that are simultaneously challenging and enriching. These activities can be completed both in school and at home to help all students learn more about their special talents and interests. To begin, let's start with a case study about a student named Ethan identified as 2eASD.

Ethan

Ethan was always considered a precocious child with intense interests and focus. When he was five years old, he was identified as having ASD. Ethan was academically advanced enough to skip a grade or two in mathematics in middle school. During middle school, Ethan learned about a devastating tornado that occurred in another state. As he watched the impacted areas recover, he began to develop an intense interest in weather and forecasting. As he first learned about the challenges associated with dangerous weather, his family was highly supportive and encouraged him to learn more. He and his parents carefully selected a weather camp that he attended in middle and high school. Over time, he became fascinated with the idea of creating an earlier warning system for severe tornadoes and has not wavered in his desire to forecast dangerous weather as his future career.

As an adult, Ethan is currently in his first year at a highly competitive university, majoring in meteorology, and acknowledges his close relationship with his family as one of the primary reasons that he has been academically successful.

So, what made Ethan so successful? Ethan explained how his interests were supported by his parents, who helped him select and finance his attendance at an independent high school that focused on 2e students. He believes that his high school did a really good job, noting that the teachers and the content prepared me well and I was really happy there. 'I made good friends, and the teachers supported my interests.' During high school, Ethan learned to advocate for his own academic needs. He honed his time management skills, explaining, 'I chunk my time out carefully and make sure that if I know I am going to need ten hours to do something, I plan to spend two hours every day on that task and then give it five days.' He believes he learned some of these skills from summer programs and the independent high school he attended. Ethan values his high school experience for teaching him social skills, enabling him to make good friends, and supporting his academic pursuits with the support of dedicated teachers and peers.

Ethan also used the social skills that he gained in high school to maintain those friendships and make new connections at his university. Being in a small and concentrated major was helpful to him, as was his ability to socialize with those in his academic cohort. He was encouraged by his teachers to develop self-advocacy skills, and he frequently uses the disabilities center for his accommodations. When asked specifically about services used in conjunction with the office, he explained that he mainly accessed extended time in math but wished 'there were more varied services for students like me.'

Why Consider Interests?

When we think about the objective of exploring and understanding student interests, we can recognize that it serves to inspire students to dedicate ample time and effort to their individual interests. As John Dewey noted in 1913, students learn best when their interests are engaged. When students develop their academic interests, they are more likely to pay attention, attend class, enroll in advanced studies, and perform well in school (Hidi and Harackiewicz, 2000). Personal interests drive students' involvement in school and influence their choices of college majors and future careers. Can you recall the first time you became passionate about something? Do you have a favorite pastime or a subject that captivates you? According to Dewey (1913), stimulating and developing students' interests begins with a positive emotional response to learning experiences. These passions serve to improve learning and engagement in school as students begin to develop their personal and academic identities.

To achieve higher engagement with your students, you may find it worthwhile to have conversations and plan activities that show your students why it is important to identify and develop interests. Some students may be unable to dedicate time and effort to the pursuit of their passions, despite enjoying them in school. Still other smart students, especially those with 2e, underachieve in school due to the challenges and frustrations that they may experience. For this reason, it is important for you to help students engage in self-reflection about their interests and talents. In this chapter, you will find several ideas and instruments that can help with these types of reflections.

Identifying Student Interests

The enrichment opportunities described in this book, including those outlined in the Schoolwide Enrichment Model (SEM), can help students examine their goals and motivations (Reis, Gelbar, and Madaus, 2021). Regardless of the grade level that you teach, it is rewarding to help students consider the steps they need to achieve their short- and long-term goals. As we know, the most effective goals typically incorporate our strengths, interests, and talents. By understanding and utilizing their abilities, students can focus on their strengths rather than perceived weaknesses. And, underachievement, a challenge facing may smart kids, can be avoided.

Using the concepts described in the SEM, teachers can guide students in creating a 'Talent Portfolio' to develop their talents in school and at home (see Appendix B). The major purposes of this type of Talent Portfolio are to

1. Regularly *collect* information about students' hobbies, interests, pastimes, extra-curricular activities, preferred methods of learning, and product preferences;
2. *Classify* this information into the general categories of abilities, interests, and learning styles;
3. Periodically *review and analyze* the information to make decisions about talent development opportunities and enrichment experiences.

When using these tools to discuss interests and abilities with students, remember that there are no right or wrong answers. We have found that students need time to consider their responses to questions about their interests, which could take a day, a week, or even longer. We have provided suggested discussions (Figures 3.1, 3.2, 3.3, and 3.4) that you can use to talk to your students about identifying their interests. We have also provided a few sample instruments for you to use with your students (see Appendices B, C, and D).

After engaging in a discussion about student interests, you might want to reiterate that not all students have defined talents, interests, or skills in a particular area. For example, as seen with Ethan, students' descriptions of their confidence in an area can reveal more than their beliefs regarding others' opinions than

---

Teacher: Everyone has special interests, abilities, and talents. *If you have a talent, that means that you have a natural ability or skill to do something well. If you have a skill in an area, other people may tell you that you are very good at that activity. Can someone share an example of a skill or interest that they have at school or at home?*	Josephine: I'm really good at math!
	Teacher: That's right, Josephine! I have noticed that you solve challenging math questions and sometimes, you even come up with new and creative ways to solve math problems! That is a great example of a skill.
	Andre: I get really good scores in English.
	Teacher: Yes, you do, Andre! I have noticed that you select books that are more challenging than what we are currently reading in class.
	Andre: I also like to write stories.
	Teacher: That's right, the stories that you write are very unique and thoughtful. Thank you for sharing!
	Kishan: I'm good at drawing, but I don't get to do that at school very much.
	Teacher: That's a great example, Kishan! You could have skills that you don't use during school, like writing songs, collecting plants, painting, or building complicated designs with legos. Others might have skills in school like computer science, leadership, or even athletics!
	Betsy: I love clowns and have always loved clowns. I have been working on a special project at home on clowns but I need help.
	Teacher: I would love to help you with this, Betsy. Why don't you tell me more about your project?

FIGURE 3.1 Learning about your Special Interests and Abilities: A Sample Classroom Discussion Part 1

their actual abilities. Encouraging students to explore their levels of confidence can encourage a deeper understanding of their strengths. This self-awareness enables them to pursue learning experiences that directly align with their interests. During these conversations, emphasize the importance of self-assessment and prioritize feelings of competence over external opinions. Remind your students to focus on learning topics and activities that *they* feel confident in, rather than those *others* tell them they are good at. This approach helps students develop self-efficacy and motivation, which are essential for personal and academic success. This discussion may naturally lead to a conversation about specific interests. A sample conversation about student interests is listed in Figure 3.2 below.

One effective way to have these conversations is through brief classroom discussions where you are receptive to their thoughts. They might talk about writing articles online, arranging shapes or colors into patterns, or working on an art piece. Some students may express musical interests, even if they do not currently play an instrument. Others might enjoy constructing things in their

---

Teacher: Everyone has talents, skills, and aptitudes. But not everyone chooses to put their effort and hard work into developing their talents and abilities. I want us to learn more about what we are interested in so that I can help show you what you need to do to get better in subjects that you are interested in! Can someone give me an example of an interest that they might have?

Andre: I like writing outside of school. I write poems.

Teacher: That's great, Andre! Your parents have told me that you have even started to write music as well! And that brings up a good point. If you are not sure what you are interested in, you might think about asking the people around you what they often find you doing.

Josephine: My parents would say that I just like to talk a lot.

Teacher: That could mean that you have oral strengths, Josephine! People with oral strengths are good at making speeches, coming up clever responses, arguing good points, and summarizing difficult material out loud. You may enjoy activities such as debate.

Kishan: What if you don't know what you're interested in?

Teacher: That's a great question, Kishan! We could learn about your abilities and interests by watching what you choose to do when you're in school. We could think about what it is that you choose to have conversations about and how you do assignments differently than other students. For example, I have noticed that you like to create visual guides when you're studying something new.

FIGURE 3.2 Learning about Your Special Interests and Abilities: A Sample Classroom Discussion Part 2

free time. Asking students to consider what they do when they have a choice will help you determine where their natural interests and talents lie. Students often prefer activities that challenge them in areas of interest, which are usually also areas where they feel successful.

You may wonder why it is important for your students to know and understand their special talents, interests, and abilities. Too often, people focus on what they or others cannot do. The purpose of enrichment in school is to help students and teachers consider what students do well and where they **want** to succeed. Developing a deeper understanding of students' talents and abilities will help them realize their potential now and in the future. Learning more about their interests can help students seek opportunities to develop their unique talents. This process can be challenging, which is why we encourage support from parents and teachers in the development of their child's interests. The case study below provides an example of students who were given the opportunity to strengthen their passions.

Young Artists United

Three young girls loved art and participated in after-school art lessons. After attending multiple classes, they came up with the idea to exhibit their work locally. Their parents encouraged this idea, thinking that organizing a display of the girls' art would help them understand the practices and challenges of professional artists. Over the next several months, their parents supported them as they created and completed several pieces each. One girl focused on sculpture, another on watercolor painting, and the third on graphite (pencil) drawing. While the girls worked on their best pieces, their parents searched for a venue. Living in a small city with only one gallery, they were disappointed but not surprised to find it unavailable. Finding a location proved frustrating until one of the parents considered his workplace. As the manager of a local Savings and Loan Bank, he had access to a large lobby that was rarely crowded. He proposed the idea of a local student art show to his Board of Directors, who were overwhelmingly supportive. The girls contacted their elementary school art teacher, who announced the opportunity to other talented students, and two more decided to join. Six months after the initial concept, the show opened with an announcement in the local newspaper and signs posted in the bank lobby. Biographies of each student accompanied their work, which were displayed on tables and cubicle walls. Many of the bank's customers made positive comments about the children's art, and the girls received several offers to purchase their pieces.

Interest Assessments

Once you have a grasp on your students' interests and talents, you can make the classroom more enjoyable and engaging, enabling you to provide enriching and challenging opportunities that leverage their strengths. In the following sections, you will find descriptions of instruments that will help you and your students explore and assess different topics of interest.

Before asking your students to complete an interest survey, it may be helpful to have a brief discussion about what it means to be interested in an activity. For example, your students might spend hours writing about self-selected topics at home but not consider creative writing an interest if they did not enjoy the last school writing assignment. Keeping this in mind, it is important to offer multiple examples to help students think differently about what it means to have an interest. A sample discussion about various interests is provided in Figure 3.3.

Below is an additional sample classroom discussion that can help you frame a conversation about student interests as you prepare them to take an interest assessment. Please note that if your school is using Renzulli Learning, this interest assessment is the first step in identifying students' interests.

At this point, your students may get excited about pursuing their identified specific interests. Your students could find it motivating to know that they will soon have the opportunity to pursue an independent study project. To prepare your students for independent or group projects, consider presenting previous examples. Further information about independent study projects, project-based learning, and implementing enrichment

Teacher: Sometimes, it can be hard for people to think about what they are interested in. If you have an interest in something, you will probably enjoy doing that activity more than you enjoy doing other things. For example, Charles Dickens loved to write and he would work on his novels for 10-12 hours every day! Think about what you enjoy doing every day. I will give you some examples.

Performing Arts: You really like music, dance, pantomime, or drama and may enjoy performing in front of someone or in a back-stage area as someone helps to direct, manage the stage or even do sets!

Writing and Journalism: You really like writing, such as fiction and non-fiction stories, prose, poetry, and recording news events.

Mathematics: You may enjoy working with numbers, problems, patterns, and logic (such as using computers, logic puzzles, word problems).

History: You may have an interest in studying the past, such as wars, famous historical figures, antiques, old photographs, ice ages, and oral histories (talking to people about their past experiences).

Fine Arts: You may like color, texture, and creating products, such as fabric, jewelry or fashion, set and costume design, and graphic layouts. You may also really be interested in photograph and furniture design.

Sciences: People who like science usually enjoy activities related to learning about biology, chemistry, environmental protection or geology and doing something with this knowledge, like experimenting or conducting a science fair project, or even collecting specimens like leaves or arrowheads.

Athletics/Sports: If you are interested in athletics or sports, you usually like physical activity, or are interested in learning about sports figures, diet, nutrition, physical therapy, or sports medicine.

Photography/Video: You may enjoy the process of producing images using photographs or making a motion picture, or even a music video, you may fall into this category.

Social Action: You may show a concern for legal, moral, or philosophical issues. You may want to change a law or do something to make the world a better place.

Business: You may show an interest in making money, organizing or starting a business, or being in a leadership role in dealing with people, such as being the play director or yearbook editor.

Technology: You may like activities that involve computers, multimedia equipment, and communication.

FIGURE 3.3 Learning about Your Special Interests and Abilities: A Sample Classroom Discussion Part 3

in your classroom is available in subsequent chapters. In a previous dialogue box, we shared a sample conversation between a teacher and a student named Betsy. This example was based on a real-life case of a student who completed an independent study project on clowns. Her story is shared in the case study below.

Betsy

Learning about clowns enabled Betsy to better understand the history of clowning which led her to read about clowning and jesters in

Teacher: We are in for a real treat today in class! Today, we are going to think about our interests and special abilities. I am going to ask you to respond to some questions by using check marks. Remember to use the check marks appropriately! I want to make sure to get the clearest picture of what it is that you like to do and what you are good at doing.	0 - If you are not interested in sports at all, mark a "0" under the Athletics/Sports question.
Some of you may be thinking, 'what if I have more than one interest?' That's exactly what this exercise is designed to help us figure out! Most people have interests in several areas. What I want you to do is to put a check mark next to a number in each of the areas that are listed on this sheet. I will go over some examples.	1 - If you are a little interested in viewing other people's photography, but not really interested in taking pictures on your own, you might mark a "1" under the Photography/Video section. This is also a good number to choose if you are not sure about how much you are interested in a subject.
	2 - If you know that there are some topics in History that you would enjoy learning more about, you might mark a "2" under the History question.
	3 - If you know that you are very interested in science, you should mark a "3" under the Science question.

FIGURE 3.4 Learning about Your Special Interests and Abilities: A Sample Classroom Discussion Part 4

European life. Understanding that many different countries and centuries could be involved in this serious study of clown history, Betsy's teacher helped her to focus again, selecting two centuries and three European countries for her research. Betsy's mother agreed to drive her to the state university to interview professors in the Fine Arts Department and to use the Fine Arts Library. Her teacher also helped her select books and articles and even learn to be a better note-taker. Over the next few months, Betsy read everything that she could find on the history of European clowning and the ways in which clowns evolved over time. With a classmate, she decided to use her knowledge to create a show that would encapsulate the history of clowns and began working on a script. In due course, the script emerged into a 45-minute show that could be presented at her school, at Girl Scouts, and any other place in which a group was gathered. Her teacher and parents helped the girls construct a small stage, and they built puppets that resembled the clowns of different centuries. As each puppet spoke, the girls realized they needed new voices to depict the history of the period. They recruited their parents, teachers, and school principal, which also resulted in increased attention for their show, titled 'Centuries of Silliness.' It was eventually shown at an assembly in their elementary school!

Student Logs

As students explore enrichment activities, they will have choices to make regarding which areas of interest they would like to pursue. To help them make these decisions, it will be helpful for them to keep a log of the enrichment activities that they find most interesting and helpful. The following log in Table 3.1 may be helpful for students as they research various sources.

After filling out this log, students will likely be able to identify two or three favorite resources that they are excited about exploring in more depth. Variations of this log can also be used for students who are developing their note-taking skills. A simplified version of the previously listed log can be found in Table 3.2 below.

Starting Small

At this point, most of your students will know what topic they are interested in pursuing. They should also have 2–3 resources that could help them explore their topic in depth. You and your students are now ready to begin the creation of a product or service that demonstrates their learning. Remember, the initial goal is not to create a big project but to allow your students to learn more about their interests. They should consider creating small group or independent projects that are appropriate in difficulty. We don't necessarily want our students to begin with projects that will take huge amounts of effort. Instead, encourage them to create smaller-scale products at first and gradually increase the scope as their skills improve. Using the information in the resources they have gathered, look back at your student's preferred method of showcasing their learning. Your students might select to try written reports, visual displays, visual guides, critical thinking games, or creative training activities, such as those discussed in the next chapter (practicing fluency, flexibility, and originality).

Some students may be overwhelmed with the thought of tackling any project at all. For these students, it might be appropriate to ask them to share what resources they prefer. You can

Identifying Students' Strengths and Interests ◆ 77

Table 3.1 Sample Enrichment Activity Student Log

Resource Name	Description	What's Good About It	What's Not Good About It	How It Connects to My Learning in School	New Ideas/Questions I Have

Table 3.2 Simplified Enrichment Activity Student Log

Resource Name	Description

encourage them to spend more time exploring and ask if they can explain why they enjoy that resource. For example, a 2e student with ADHD might prefer an audiobook that enables them to listen to content throughout their day. The versatility of these learning experiences will allow your students to succeed regardless of their academic abilities.

Some students might still struggle with choosing one area to explore, especially if they have found several topics or areas that interest them. For these students, you might consider some guidance, such as pointing them to a resource that you know will interest them. For instance, if you know a few of your students are interested in animals, you might suggest exploring the topic of mammals in depth. You might share the following subtopics or starting points to help expand their understanding of mammals: (a) mammal experts; (b) mammals in the woods; (c) marine mammals. You can ask your students to find at least one online resource database about mammals and share what they found. If your students respond well to this prompt, consider asking them to craft a greeting card about the animal they have selected. Alternatively, they may want to think about creating a small pop-up book about the mammal. A more advanced project could involve creating an infographic about different types of mammals, including pictures of various species, descriptions of their habitats, the food they eat, and any other pertinent information. Researching topics of interest should be enjoyable, not overwhelming. If your students need to pursue their interests at a less intimidating level, show them how. If they want to delve deeper, encourage them to do so. Remind your students that it is okay to set goals that they feel are appropriate for them, in turn allowing them to develop the confidence to become experts in their chosen topics.

See below for another example of a project that demonstrates how far some students can go when they are really interested in a topic.

Mentors for Technology

The educational experience of three middle school girls was changed dramatically when they attended a seminar that featured women in high-tech positions. The speakers at the talk discussed gender equity, cultural attitudes, and the barriers faced by women in STEM fields. When they left the seminar, the trio could not stop talking about what they had learned. They began to explore websites and online resources to learn about the challenges faced by women in computer science and engineering. They discovered fascinating facts about female technology pioneers, reading compelling biographies of inspirational women, from Rosalind Franklin to Ada Augusta Lovelace. With their parents' and teachers' support, the girls decided to conduct an advanced research project on a female pioneer in STEM of their choosing.

The girls learned that while women hold just 25% of all professional IT positions in America, they bring invaluable skills to technology organizations. Inspired by a study of professional women who have changed power structures in the corporate world, the young women began developing a tech-based workshop to share with younger girls in their district. To facilitate this, they found a network that allowed them to set up a virtual classroom for discussions and idea exchanges. Their earlier research on women in STEM fields helped them refine their focus and determine the most useful applications for their new mentor program. They developed a range of activities to engage the younger girls, including the program with a presentation highlighting the achievements of eminent women scientists and technology pioneers, emphasizing that 'Science, Math, Engineering, and Technology Can Be Fun!' The students engaged in 'tinkering activities' and 'artistic play,' designing colorful messages, flashing marquees, pop-up buttons, and vibrant text effects. These experiences led to an increased enrollment of young women in the local computer science summer camp.

The Interest-A-Lyzer

Appendices A–D provide examples of popular interest surveys that teachers use to identify both their interests and those of their students. For example, in Appendix C, *If I Ran the School*, students are asked to consider which activities they would like to learn about if they were in charge of creating curricula for their school. In this survey, students can choose 10 items, which can help teachers gather information about the range of interests that may motivate their class. Appendices D and E, *Interest-A-Lyzer and Primary Interest-A-Lyzer*, are tools for K-6 students to share their interests and ideas. The surveys invite students to consider their favorite topics and emphasize that there are no right or wrong answers regarding their interests.

The *Interest-A-Lyzer* also provides teachers with information that can be used to plan learning activities to help students explore their interests. For example, if you know that one of your students has a potential interest in journalism, you can encourage them to pursue this interest, which will eventually lead to them development of an independent or small group project. We will discuss this further in Chapter 4. See Appendix D for additional questions that you may use with students to learn about their interests.

Conclusion

Exploring the interests of your students is an inherently strength-based activity, as many interest surveys ask students to reflect on what they are good at and enjoy doing. It is important that teachers determine what students are interested in as these interests can reveal the nature of students' specific academic gifts and talents. When students are genuinely interested in a topic or activity, they will be more inclined to rehearse and practice skills related to that area. In the regular prescriptive curriculum, students may never be allowed to demonstrate their skills in areas they find personally enjoyable. This is why it is so important for you as an educator to come alongside your students and remind them that their interests matter. The confidence and joy students gain from learning about a topic they love will enhance their abilities and strengthen their desire to demonstrate their intellectual potential.

References

Dewey, J. (1913). *Interest and Effort in Education.* Houghton Mifflin Company. https://doi.org/10.1037/14633-000

Hidi, S., and Harackiewicz, J. M. (2000). Motivating the academically unmotivated: A critical issue for the 21st century. *Review of Educational Research*, 70(2), 151–179. https://doi.org/10.3102/00346543070002151

Reis, S. M., Gelbar, N. W., and Madaus, J. W. (2021). Understanding the academic success of academically talented college students with autism spectrum disorders. *Journal of Autism and Developmental Disorders.* https://doi.org/10.1007/s10803-021-05290-4

4

Planning Enrichment Experiences That Work for All Students

Can you remember when you first fell in love with a hobby? When you first became inspired to pursue a specific interest or career? At some point in our lives, most of us are exposed to a topic that sparks our interest. For you, it may have been an especially compelling class or lecture in college, someone you admired who shared their work with you, or a place you visited that made an impression on you. Perhaps it was a teacher who guided you through a difficult lesson or learning experience, or a place you visited with family or friends. Regardless, specific memories will hold a special place in your heart for a number of reasons. For many students, childhood memories like these can be incredibly motivating as they consider how their decisions influence on who they will become.

The Enrichment Triad Model, the curricular core of the larger SEM, provides the building blocks for these memories. An overview of the SEM is included in Figure 4.1. Traditionally, the SEM has been used to organize services provided to gifted students. However, the components of the SEM may also be used to identify and nurture the academic needs of students demonstrating a wide variety of abilities, including 2e students. By using the model, teachers are able to provide their students with opportunities to identify their strengths and engage in enriching learning opportunities.

DOI: 10.4324/9781003511861-4

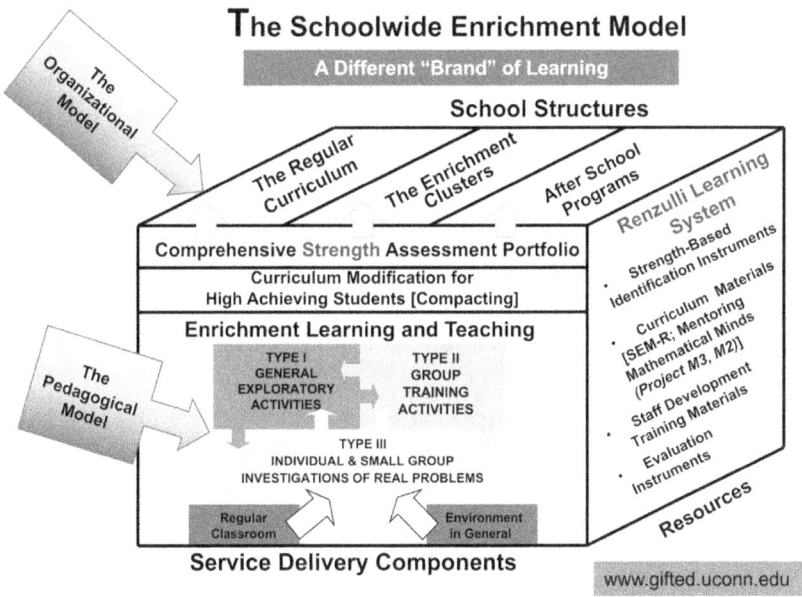

FIGURE 4.1 The Schoolwide Enrichment Model

Embedded in the core of the SEM is the Enrichment Triad Model with its three types of enrichment. *Type I Enrichment* exposes students to topics that can excite and engage them in a variety of ways that would not ordinarily be covered in the curriculum; *Type II Enrichment* provides training to develop thinking and feeling processes through the use of different materials and methods; and *Type III Enrichment* enables students to improve their skills in a self-selected area of interest, often through the development of a specific product (Renzulli and Reis, 1997). A visual depiction of each type and their interaction with each other is provided in Figure 4.2.

Many educators have embraced the Enrichment Triad Model as a tool to enhance the educational experiences of all students. It is important to note that we need to provide these types of opportunities to every child, rather than only those identified as having talents. Neurodiverse and 2e students often have numerous talents that go unrecognized because their disabilities mask these strengths (Reis, Baum, and Burke, 2014). Current research, however, demonstrates that these students are highly capable of

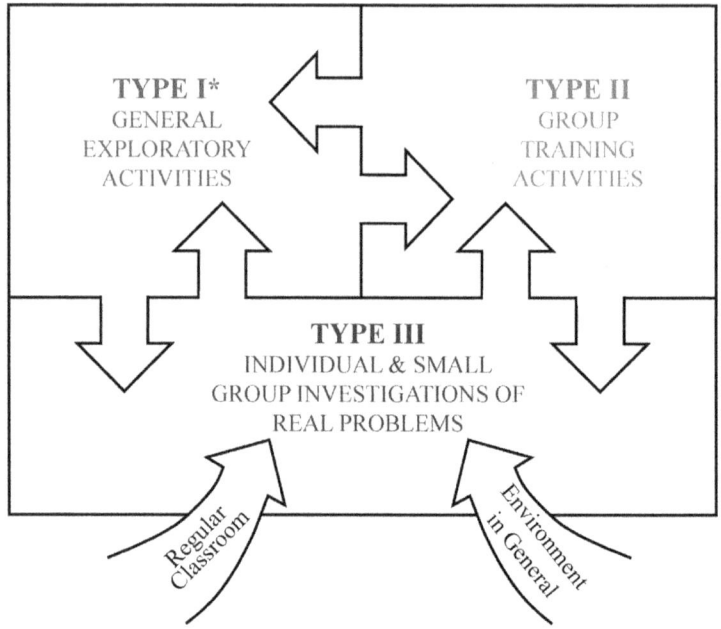

FIGURE 4.2 The Enrichment Triad Model

pursuing interest-based extracurricular activities and participating in challenging classes (Madaus et al., 2023; Reis, Renzulli, and Renzulli, 2021; Reis, Gelbar, and Madaus, 2022; Reis and Peters, 2021). Too often, individuals with strong potential to self-improve are be overlooked for enrichment activities.

Think of a student in your classroom who demonstrates a heightened interest in a particular topic, activity, or idea. This student might be recognized as talented or have special education needs. Alternatively, they might not have been identified for either. Consider the energy that this student brings to their personal interests. How would students like them respond to opportunities in the classroom to explore their interests? For students who are not particularly interested in any activity they complete in the classroom, what changes would you expect to see if they became excited about a topic? Could they be more motivated or successful? What about more engaged? Experiences organized around the Enrichment Triad Model enable this growth and benefit all types of learners, regardless of their present levels of achievement.

If you use the Enrichment Triad Model in your classroom, you may be able to accomplish several important goals. First, you can provide enrichment to all students by expanding the types of experiences that they have in school (Type I). Second, you may glean information that enables you to make meaningful decisions about how to further organize activities that develop students' thinking and doing skills (Type II). Finally, you may be able to stimulate students' interests in more intensive (Type III) follow-up activities, such as projects or products. This chapter offers guidance about:

1. How to use the Enrichment Triad Model to guide strength-based learning;
2. Various types of enrichment and how they can work within the classroom;
3. Organizing Types I, II, and III Enrichment activities in the classroom;
4. How to use the Enrichment Triad Model to maintain students' engagement and motivation in academic activities.

Bringing Type I into General Education and Special Education Classrooms

The types of planning you do during Type I will largely determine the success of the other components of the Enrichment Triad Model. Many students want to pursue areas of personal interest but may not know how. You have likely noticed that some of your students, although they demonstrate high levels of ability, become bored with regular curriculum and are easily distracted. You may know students who refuse to engage in topics that are not related to their specific interests. These students may have been diagnosed with ADHD or ASD, and share a unique need to explore very particular areas of interest (Reis, Baum, and Burke, 2014). Offering Type I experiences can help your 2e students realize that the classroom can be an exciting and engaging space.

Researchers have found that students who have ASD and high potential have usually gained specific strengths that equip them for success in college and other post-high school opportunities (Madaus et al., 2023). Many of these strengths include high levels of intrinsic motivation, resilience, and coping skills, all of which are typically heightened by academic interest. For example, a 2e student with ADHD may struggle to sustain motivation on a reading task outside of their area of interest. However, this motivation might increase dramatically when they are presented with a task that incorporates a topic of passion. Often, the biggest challenges for these students become their greatest assets when given the right opportunities and resources. By actively working to increase focus and endurance in our classroom, we can use the resilience of 2e students combined with their interests to keep them motivated.

You may have been provided with directive curriculum materials and policies that stifle creative differences in your classroom. For too long, the predominant school culture has been guided by deficit-based perspectives, where differences imply failure and conformity is key. Using the SEM means you are implementing a strength-based approach to learning opportunities with your students. Planning Type I experiences in the classroom will provide opportunities for growth, especially given the diversity of experiences, personalities, and abilities that exist among your students. For over four decades, Renzulli and Reis have argued that students are more engaged when they have an opportunity to build upon their strengths. Our research, outlined in this book, has highlighted the importance of strength-based strategies to enable students to maximize their skills and increase their engagement.

The SEM recognizes that each learner is unique and that learning becomes more effective when students enjoy their activities. It is likely that a strength-based perspective is not new to many teachers, especially to those who are experienced. It is, however, possible that teachers who believe in teaching to students' strengths may not be aware of specific strategies. We provide several suggestions for these, including some that are a part of the original SEM and others that have emerged in the research discussed in this book. In our experience, teachers often demonstrate their understanding and openness to the characteristics of 2e students, but many do not have access to best practices for supporting each student's unique needs. In this chapter, we will provide teachers with a few tools to accommodate students' diverse needs.

Type I Enrichment and Strength-Based Learning

Type I Enrichment experiences can be easily implemented in classrooms as a strength-based strategy. This approach allows teachers to focus on students' strengths, identify their interests, and provide experiences that help them succeed (Reis et al., 2022). When students participate in enrichment activities, they recognize their talents, which builds thier confidence in their academic abilities. Type I Enrichment, part of the Enrichment Triad Model (Renzulli, 1977) and embedded into the SEM, exposes students to various topics and encourages them to explore self-selected areas of interest. In this way, the SEM is inherently strength-based, as it enables teachers to provide student choice in ways that enhance learning.

For many of your students, the Type I experiences you facilitate will be the first time they have experienced a strength-based educational opportunity. This is especially true for your students who have been identified with disabilities and may be at risk for developing negative academic self-concepts that are associated with deficit-based instruction (Reis, McGuire, and Neu, 2000). These inclusive education practices have been welcomed into a variety of educational settings, including classrooms, after school programs, Saturday enrichment opportunities, and special education settings. Without strength-based strategies, your 2e students may compare themselves to their neurotypical classmates and worry that they do not measure up.

It is especially common for students from diverse cultural backgrounds to encounter deficit-based perspectives in their educational settings. Fortunately, the strength-based nature of the SEM encourages inclusive practices for all students and has been used to provide challenging curricula for students who have been historically underrepresented in enrichment programs. Additionally, students from low-income homes benefit greatly from exposure to a broad range of topics (Kaul et al., 2015), which is a fundamental component of a Type I Enrichment experience. When you implement the Enrichment Triad Model, your students can explore topics that are meaningful to their unique experiences and cultures while pursuing projects that allow them to engage in the classroom.

Type I Enrichment: Where to Start?

The SEM is a popular approach to providing enrichment opportunities for students and has been used in thousands of schools both nationally and internationally (Reis and Peters, 2021). Depending on your resources you may or may not have access to an enrichment specialist available to help you plan Type I Enrichment experiences. If you do, take advantage of their support. If not, many teachers have implemented stimulating Type I Enrichment programs without specialist guidance.

As you start preparing for Type I Enrichment, consider which students might benefit the most. Research shows that the SEM is effective in providing equal access to challenging curricula (Allen et al., 2016; Reis and Peters, 2021), but you might identity certain students or groups of students with more more immediate needs. This group could serve as your initial target audience for a Type I experience.

When starting, think about where the first Type I experience should take place. The students you select as your target audience for a Type I experience will help determine this initial location. Type I experiences can be offered to specific grade levels, students across grades, or even the entire school. These experiences can occur anywhere, including inside the school, at museums, or even in students' homes. You might find it helpful to start with a small group of students before attempting a larger-scale Type I experience. On the other hand, you may enjoy the external support of organizing a broader experience. Your role as a teacher is crucial to the success of Type I planning, so it is important to plan for activities that are best suited to your needs and preferences.

Brainstorming Type I Topics: Students

Joseph Renzulli described Type I Enrichment activities as catalysts for curiosity and internal motivation, suggesting that 'Type

I enrichment may be the method for externally stimulating students toward internal commitment and purpose' (2012, p. 155). According to Renzulli, exploratory activities go beyond exposing students to new topics. They can also introduce students to new problems, issues, ideas, notions, theories, and skills. More importantly, Type I Enrichment experiences will open students' imaginations to make room for new possibilities. For some of your students, it could be helpful to draw these concepts from the interests that have already captured their attention.

You will likely already be aware of some of your students' interests. These passions can often be seen in what they choose to do with their time both inside and outside the classroom. Can you think of a lesson that was particularly engaging to most of your students? Maybe your students were invested in an astronomy lesson or moved during a reading of *The Giving Tree*. A Type I experience could involve isolating a specific aspect of these lessons and beginning an exploration with activities that require increasing depth and complexity.

Although you may have a good grasp on what sorts of topics are particularly engaging to your students, it is still worthwhile to assess their individual passions. Students of various ability levels will require educational approaches that build upon their particular strengths and interests, many of which may not be apparent in a whole-class activity. Use interest surveys such as *If I Ran the School* (see Appendix C) or the *Interest-A-Lyzer* (see Appendix D and Appendix E) to gauge your students' potential areas of interest. You might also conduct a whole-class discussion about interests. Questions such as 'What is worth knowing?' and 'What are some things that you wonder about?' could prompt students to generate topics that they would not have otherwise considered.

In some schools that use the SEM, students are able to participate in *enrichment clusters*. These are groups of students who share common interests and work together with an adult during specially designated time blocks. Organizing enrichment clusters has been shown to improve students' awareness of their roles in the schools and their surrounding communities. This may be especially beneficial for students who struggle to form social bonds with their peers (as many of our 2e students do). We will discuss more about enrichment clusters later.

If I ran the school

A PRIMARY INTEREST INVENTORY
developed by Deborah E. Burns
designed by Del Siegle

Name _____

Grade _____ Teacher _____

If I ran the school, I would choose to learn about these ten things. I have thought about my answers very carefully and I have circled my best ideas for right now.

I am really interested in:

1. The Stars and Planets
2. Birds
3. Dinosaurs and Fossils
4. Life in the Ocean
5. Trees, Plants and Flowers
6. The Human Body
7. Monsters and Mysteries
8. Animals and Their Homes
9. Outer Space, Astronauts, and Rockets
10. The Weather
11. Electricity, Light, and Energy
12. Volcanoes and Earthquakes
13. Insects
14. Reptiles
15. Rocks and Minerals
16. Machines and Engines
17. Diseases and Medicine
18. Chemistry and Experiments

1. Families
2. The Future
3. Our Presidents
4. The United States
5. Other Countries
6. History and Long Ago Times
7. Famous Men and Women
8. Problems We Have in Our Town
9. Holidays
10. Native Americans, Asian Americans, Hispanics and African Americans
11. Explorers
12. People Who Live and Work in Our Town
13. Travel and Transportation

FIGURE 4.3 Sample of If I Ran the School

If I Ran the School...page 2

1. Math Games and Puzzlers
2. Measuring Lines, Liquids, Weight
3. Shapes and Sizes
4. Buying and Money
5. Calculators and Computers
6. Building
7. Counting and Numbering
8. Calendars and Time
9. Math Stories and Problems

1. Writing a Book
2. Writing Poems
3. Writing Plays and Skits
4. Writing Newspapers
5. Making Speeches
6. Sign Language
7. Making a Book
8. Comic and Cartoon Strips
9. Letter Writing
10. Spanish and French
11. Talking and Listening to Stories
12. Making a New Game or Puzzle

1. Cartoons
2. Art Projects
3. Painting
4. Clay
5. Acting
6. Dancing
7. Drawing
8. Writing Music
9. Photography
10. Movies
11. Puppets
12. Radio and Television
13. Famous Artists and Their Work
14. Making New Toys
15. Magic
16. Mime

1. Doctors
2. Lawyers
3. Police Work
4. Fire Fighters
5. Scientists
6. Builders
7. Reporters
8. Store Workers
9. Sports Stars
10. Actors
11. Veterinarians
12. Farmers
13. Writers
14. Engineers
15. Artists
16. Inventors

You forgot to list some of my very special interests. They are: _____

FIGURE 4.3 (Continued)

Brainstorming Type I Topics: School Staff and Families

Remember that high-quality Type I topics and experiences will benefit both your current and future students. Collaborate with your colleagues to create a storage system for Type I data and ideas. This could be an online list or directory of Type I topics, experiences, and opportunities. Use this space to store ideas that have sparked student interest, such as museum brochures, blogs, or biographies of local artists. You might create a virtual space like a Pinterest board or Google Drive folder to hold your personal inspirations. You can keep these folders private or share them with colleagues, and even invite them to collaborate to quickly brainstorm Type I topics and share resources.

Consider reaching out to your students' parents and guardians for potential Type I topics. Just as you and your colleagues have a wealth of experiences to guide Type I planning, so too might your students' families. Many family members are interested in participating in their child's education and could become enthusiastic supporters of your Type I Enrichment plans. Caregivers might share their experiences in a Type I activity or have contacts who can offer such experiences. This is also an opportunity for students to explore their diverse cultural backgrounds, as caregivers might present culturally significant Type I activities. This approach fosters multigenerational connections, as caregivers may know older family members or friends who would like to share their stories and expertise with your class.

Brainstorming Type I Topics: Outside of the School

It may be easier than you think to expand the use of Type I topics beyond your school. Many public agencies, professional organizations, and community groups already visit schools for presentations and are eager to educate young people about their associations. Available resources will vary based on your community but could include local fire departments, park services, historical societies, or diversity organizations. In addition to inviting speakers to visit your classroom, you may consider visiting cultural and scientific areas or vocational institutions.

Similarly, college and university staff can be valuable sources of information and inspiration for Type I Enrichment experiences.

Contacting a local university's office of public information may give you insight into the various speakers, visitations, and special events that are of interest to you and your students. College students are a source that might be helpful, as they are often enthusiastic about creating ties in the community and may be looking for professional experiences. If you do not have a university that is within a reasonable distance of your school, virtual universities may have online resources that you can share with your students.

Local retailers and businesses are also possible sources of authentic Type I experiences. These businesses may have ties to students' guardians, which may become apparent in conversations with families. Oftentimes, these businesses can direct you to outreach programs and resources that could serve as Type I experiences. When planning Type I activities, speak to your student's parents and families. More often than not, they will have connections that can support your goals and plans.

Brainstorming Type I Topics: Virtual Discovery

In the digital era, you have likely honed your skills in finding quality educational resources for your students online. You and the other teachers in your school or district may already have an inventory of websites that you use on a regular basis. If so, it may be useful to scour those websites for possible Type I Enrichment topics. If not, you may find it useful to select and explore a few internet sources for topics and Type I experiences that may be of interest to your students. If you're struggling to know where to start, remember to go back to the data you collected with your interest surveys. Many organizations have freely available learning resources and guides for students and educators that you can easily incorporate into your plan. Some of these resources include:

- **Space to Learn: Learning Resources from the National Aeronautics and Space Administration** (NASA; www.nasa.gov/learning-resources/)
- **Ideas for Books, Videos, and Websites to Teach Students about National Parks** (https://education.nationalgeographic.org/resource/national-park-resources/)

- **The Metropolitan Museum Learning Guides** (www.metmuseum.org/learn/kids-and-families/family-guides)
- **A Collection of Images, Recordings, Texts, and Videos from the Smithsonian** (https://learninglab.si.edu/search/?f%5B_types%5D%5B%5D=ll_collection&s=updated_at_desc&page=1&mm&mm_op&mm_t)
- **A List of Writing Contests** (https://imaginationsoup.net/writing-contests-kids-ways-get-published/)

Remember that your students have also developed skills while searching the internet for resources. Ask students to recommend some of the websites that they enjoy exploring and determine if these could serve as Type I experiences for other students. Not all of the recommendations will strike you as a high-quality educational resource, but keep in mind that you are only trying to brainstorm topics at this stage of your efforts. Try to keep an open mind as your students share their findings with you.

Many of your students may be passionate about computer science or video games. These are easy areas of interest that you can harness to create unique educational experiences. Researchers are reconceptualizing their approach to game design to identify ways to effectively engage learners at various cognitive levels through game-based learning (Plass, Homer, and Kinzer, 2015). It is possible that the games your students enjoy today will transform into quality educational activities in the future. Understanding the value of games can bring incredible benefits to your classroom. The recommendations that your students share with you will give you insight into what they doing with their free time, which can help you to examine possible Type I Enrichment topics. We have provided an example of a student who discovered their topic of interest after watching a television program in the following case study.

Allison

When Allison, a seventh grader, became interested in researching the colors of the stars after watching a program on NOVA, her parents were unsure where to turn. Having no background whatsoever in this area, they decided to contact someone from a local astronomy club. This led to a few chats with a local astronomer who volunteered to work with Allison as a mentor and directed her to a local science center where she found a group of students her age. Together, they attended several night visits to the science center's small planetarium, and Allison began to learn about the colors of the stars. As she learned how astronomers photograph the stars to study their spectra, she became increasingly invested. The teacher leading the young astronomy group suggested a call to a local space research center. To Allison's delight, she was able to find another mentor who lent her a camera that could be connected to a high-powered telescope at a nearby university. Her parents coordinated with local university professors to enable Allison to use the telescope, and under the watchful eyes of doctoral students, she finished her work. When her classroom teachers learned about her project, they encouraged Allison to submit her work to the State Science Fair, where she ultimately won a first-place certificate.

Planning Type I Topics

Consider all of these ideas as you plan Type I Enrichment experiences. As you organize activities in the Enrichment Triad Model, it may be useful to ask students to reflect on whether their interest in the topic increased or decreased throughout their experiences. This may be indicative of which topics are able to sustain the most attention for the longest amount of time.

With so many potential topics to choose from, you may wonder where to begin. It is important to understand that there is no one right way to start providing enrichment experiences. Enrichment experiences have been associated with both increased academic achievement and positive socioemotional outcomes for students, so you can rest assured that your students will benefit from your efforts no matter which topic they choose. For example, one study found that students' attendance rates improved on days when enrichment experiences were offered, regardless of whether enrichment experiences pertaining to their personal interests were selected (Allen et al., 2016).

Example of Type I

To begin brainstorming, we will explore a Type I Enrichment experience through the lens of a seventh-grade science teacher.

If you were to put yourself in the place of this teacher, you may wish to provide an interdisciplinary enrichment opportunity for your students. STEAM (Science, Technology, Engineering, Arts, and Mathematics) projects and activities challenge students to develop their creative talents and thinking skills (Coxon and Cody, 2022; Madden et al., 2013). Remember, some students are interested in developing their creative skills and participating in STEAM opportunities, so consider them as you develop Type I Enrichment topics.

You and your family recently visited the Wadsworth Atheneum Museum of Art in Hartford, Connecticut. You found the exhibits fascinating and believe your students would find them equally engaging. Searching their website, you discover several educational opportunities for students, including virtual guided tours, teacher-guided visits, and studio program videos. One studio program video, 'STEAM: Sketch Like a Scientist,' is recommended for students in grades 6–12. This program includes a pre-recorded 15–20 minute gallery tour and art demonstrations that you can view at your convenience. Due to the subject and flexibility of this option, you decide to request a link to this experience.

You inform other teachers that you will be sharing this video with your students. Depending on interest, you may show the art exhibit in your classroom or request a larger space from your principal to host multiple classrooms. Fortunately, the program is flexible, allowing you to use it whenever possible. For this example, you discuss the Type I Enrichment experience with your principal, who agrees to help you present the video in the school auditorium. Teachers of all subjects and grade levels are invited to attend.

In another Type I experience, teachers from a certain grade level invited a speaker from a local Audobon Society to speak about local challenges regarding conservation, and what we can learn from birds. The content of the talk focused on the global effort to identify habitat that will protect sustainable populations of birds. The other focus of the talk on preserving our environment discussed how the Audobon Society and other conservation partners make conservation decisions in the face of considerable uncertainty from the changing climate, the economy, and gaps in our knowledge of the abundance and distribution of our highest priority species of birds. Many of the 65 students who attended the talk were very interested in the content but there were a few students who ran up to the speaker at the end of the talk with multiple questions.

Type I: Debriefing
Whether the Type I experience occurs in a single classroom or across multiple rooms, it is important to gauge students' interest by facilitating discussions about the activity. Consider sending an email to the students' caregivers to share information about the Type I experience and offer suggestions for extending the students' learning at home. Some of your student's parents and guardians may not be aware of available resources they can use to cultivate their child's interest in a subject. For the example above, the Wadsworth Museum website provides virtual studio art packs for children who are interested in learning more about the significance of symbols, alternative angles, and surreal scenes. Sharing these resources with caregivers will help you reinforce positive communication with families and increase the likelihood that students will explore their interests beyond the school day. In the other Type I discussed, the speaker from the Audobon Society patiently answered questions, invited some of the most interested students to visit with their parents and families, and provided links to future talks and ways in which the students could become more actively involved.

Type I experiences should mark the beginning of an educational adventure, not the end. While discussing the experience with your students, be on the lookout for those who show a keen interest in a given subject. Offer opportunities for students to share their feedback in different way, such as through exit tickets, one-on-one teacher meetings, or thumbs-up/thumbs-down strategies. Some of your students may be unable or unwilling to demonstrate interest in the same ways as their peers, so make sure you offer multiple comfortable methods for them to share their thoughts. Other Type I exposure activites include:

- ◆ Virtual fieldtrips
- ◆ Real fieldtrips

- Movies and streamingBooks (Non-fiction, fiction, etc.)
- Online activites
- Contests and competitions

Type I Experiences: Special Considerations

You may be wondering if there are some students who should not engage in a Type I Enrichment experience. While it is understandable to have concerns about which students will be participating in initial Type I activities, it is important to focus on developing the personal interests of *all* students in your classroom. These educational opportunities are beneficial to every student, regardless of their needs and abilities. Each student deserves an opportunity to experience the positive outcomes that are associated with enrichment opportunities. Fiddyment (2014) explored the perceptions of various teachers who facilitated enrichment experiences in their classrooms. In this study, students who had high academic, emotional, and behavioral support needs were able to participate in various enrichment activities that focused on topics including art, cooking, and physical education. The researchers found that behavior issues were minimized during the enrichment experience because students were highly engaged. Additionally, they observed that students with higher needs were able to fully participate in the activity when teachers took their interests into careful consideration. Reis, Gentry and Maxfield (1998) also explored the inclusion of students with behavioral challenges in enrichment opportunities, finding that behavior problems were significantly reduced or eliminated when students had choice about which enrichment experiences they pursued.

If you have concerns about whether a particular student will disrupt the learning of others, think about ways to provide an enrichment opportunity that would be both manageable and meaningful. You could provide activities for students to explore independently through links to virtual art tours or allow them to practice using different types of art materials. You should still consider placing this student in an enrichment cluster based on their personal interest, as they may interact differently with a small group of like-minded peers.

Type II Enrichment and Strength-Based Learning

The next stage of the Enrichment Triad Model involves the use of Type II Enrichment. As a reminder, Type II Enrichment focuses on the development of process skills and instructional methods that bolster critical thinking, problem-solving, and decision-making. These activities are designed to help students acquire and apply advanced skills necessary for independent investigation and research. Drawing student interest into a topic is an important step in the SEM process, so when you are ready to move beyond Type I Enrichment experiences to Type II Enrichment experiences, it is important for you to recognize the value of what you have already contributed to your students' education. Once you have your students hooked on a specific topic of interest, it is time to help them develop the skills that they will need to pursue their goals. Teachers are encouraged to use pedagogical practices that emphasize 21st-century skills to promote inclusive, equitable, and quality educational opportunities for all learners (González-Pérez and Ramírez-Montoya, 2022). This typically involves designing educational activities that develop creativity, critical thinking, cognitive and interpersonal skills, social and civic competence, and responsible citizenship. Using Type II activities in the classroom will support students' acquisition of these life skills.

During their exploration of self-selected topics, students will need to engage in creative problem-solving, critical thinking, and decision-making. They will also develop affective skills such as sensing, appreciating, and evaluating, along with research skills like note-taking, interviewing, analyzing, and reviewing. Additionally, students may enhance their written, oral, and visual communication skills related to their investigations. These skills can be developed simultaneously as students engage in Type II investigations. While the specific skills and materials for Type II training will vary depending on your students' interest, the next sections will provide you with examples of how to conduct Type II Enrichment experiences in your classroom. Some Type II activities, such as those incorporating creative thinking and problem-solving, are appropriate for all students. However, more advanced activities may be better suited for students with academic talents or for students or those with high interests in a topic.

Encouraging new skills in the classroom can involve the use of Type II Enrichment activities. It is easy to focus on students' deficits while creating opportunities that highlight their interests and abilities is more challenging. Implementing Type II Enrichment in your classroom makes it easier to create strengths-based learning, which will positively affect the learning dynamic in your classroom. When students see the relevance of their academic success to their personal interests, they find school to be more meaningful (Gubbins, 1995). Providing Type II Enrichment opportunities demonstrates your confidence in them.

From the beginning, the Enrichment Triad Model has been accessible to students who exhibit a variety of interests, needs, and abilities and the group training activities used in Type II Enrichment are no exception. Type II Enrichment experiences should be designed to reflect your student's needs and offer scaffolding for students who wish to pursue self-selected areas of interest. Often, these activities involve personal challenges, but by engaging in these experiences in an intellectually safe environment, students are able to meaningfully embrace productive struggle.

When starting a Type II Enrichment experience, the activities conducted with your class will depend on your individual students and their prior learning. Type II activities often involve advanced instruction in students' self-selected areas of interest (Reis et al., 2014). The skills most beneficial for your students to develop should be related to these areas of interest.

There are a variety of skills included in the *Taxonomy of Type II Enrichment Processes* created by Joe Renzulli and depicted in Figure 4.4 below.

Within each of these skill areas, there are a number of smaller, interrelated steps that require scaffolding. For example, within the 'learning how-to-learn skills' category, students might need to work on their ability to listen, observe, and perceive. One of your students may have trouble evaluating a speaker's point of view, so you may decide it would be helpful for them to make inferences instead. If they continue to struggle, it could be beneficial to have them practice a different, related skill, such as describing important details. As students become more confident in one

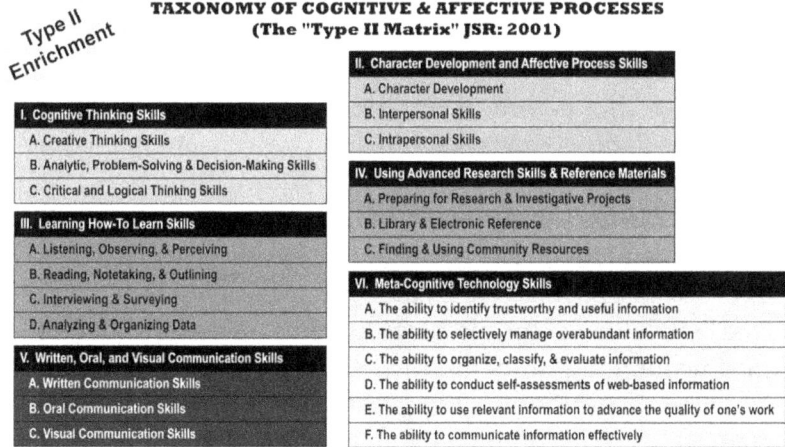

FIGURE 4.4 Taxonomy of Type II Enrichment Processes

skill, they will feel more comfortable tackling areas they find challenging. This approach encourages students to explore different subtopics at levels that are appropriately challenging for them.

Type II Enrichment: Where to Start?

Given that your students' self-selected areas of interest may vary significantly, it may be helpful to consider offering different Type II activities. This will make it easier to prepare for pre-planned Type II activities while remaining flexible in the event that your students demonstrate more intense levels of interest in a given topic. Type II activities in each dimension offer authentic enrichment experiences that you can implement to meet your students' needs.

Pre-planned Type II activities are systematic enrichment opportunities for students in particular grade levels or groups. The activities that we will be discussing in this chapter are examples of this first dimension of Type II activities. The second kind of Type II activities involves methodological skills that stem from students' interests in a subject, including how to do something. These interests could emerge from regular curricular lessons, experiences outside of school, or previously offered Type I Enrichment opportunities. Finally, Type II activities can also relate to specific Type III Enrichment options. If students are interested in pursuing Type III Enrichment activities, they may need training before they begin. Because of this, Type II training can be seen as a period of preparation. Allowing your students to practice various processes and skills will ensure that your students are able to be successful in their future projects.

Some methodological skills will relate to Type I experiences that your students have enjoyed. For example, for the students who were fascinated by the Audobon experience that was organized, introducing simple birdwatching methods skills will be fun. Encouraging students to find the 'how to' of next steps will bring them to several great resources, including their state botanical gardens or their Audobon Societies, but inevitably, Type II skills in this area will include getting a field guide, such as *Peterson's First Guide to Birds of North America*, a perfect pocket sized guide for a beginning birder. Next, would be using a camera or a digital camera and taking photos that can be checked on a site such as Cornell Lab's free Merlin Bird ID. Bird watchers also take notes and record their observations, such as the bird's size and shape, color patterns, and behaviors. Watchers can record both questions as well as personal observations to research later. Starting a bird watching journal also makes things fun and encouraging kids to colored pencils or crayons to doodle and make observations can be really enjoyable. So, can listening and encouraging students to get the Merlin Bird app to listen to sounds that they can then identify is an excellent way to encourage critical thinking. We also encourage understanding the tools and vocabulary of the trade! So, trying to borrow binoculars to use and learning the vocabulary that goes with bird watching is also important—focus, field of vision, and so on!

Think about the skills that students can acquire from this Type II training, including patience, critical thinking, problem-solving, observation, note-taking, journaling, and research. And the list goes on! It might take you only a few minutes to find the best how-to sites for your students to learn these types of skills!

The more often you implement components in the SEM, the more your own skills will improve. When you begin your SEM efforts, it may make the most sense for you to plan Type

II activities in advance, which can and should be done as you are thinking about Type I Enrichment activities. Your students may demonstrate an interest in a particular subject following their engagement in a Type I experience, so it is likely that your pre-planned Type II experience will be compatible with your students' developing interests. Over time (or once you feel comfortable) you will likely find it easier to adapt your Type II Enrichment activities to your students' interests.

Organizing Type II Enrichment Activities

Remember to recognize the skills you already have related to Type II training activities. More than likely, you already have experience teaching your students many core processes and thinking skills. For example, your class may have already engaged in activities that allow them to practice processing skills including reading, outlining, or writing. These activities may allow students to practice some of the skills that they have applied during previous lessons. You may choose to practice Type II process skills that you have never taught before, which could include interviewing, surveying, or organizing data. Regardless of the skills that you focus on, you should feel confident that what you have already taught will help you and your students to meaningfully engage in Type II training.

As with Type I Enrichment activities, it is helpful to keep a record of the Type II Enrichment activities that have been successful in your classroom. If these experiences are beneficial to one group of students, they will likely be useful for future classes and may also help students in other classrooms. If you know a teacher in your school or district who is implementing the SEM, collaborating on activities that have worked in your respective classrooms can be advantageous. Other staff members, especially those teaching the same grade level or content area, can support your Type II training efforts.

Consider creating a space, either physical or virtual, where you and your colleagues can collaborate. Share links to educational books, videos, or podcasts that focus on Type II skills. Provide suggestions for using these materials and accommodations for students with learning challenges. Assign someone to keep the collection up to date and replace any inaccessible resources. Be flexible with your collection of Type II materials, as there is no right or wrong way to select and implement these resources.

Type II Enrichment Activities: Group and Individual Opportunities

Different subjects require specific thinking skills and problem-solving for projects and homework. For this reason, the decisions you make about the Type II processes that your students will practice may largely be determined by the regular curriculum topics and unit sequences that are already in place. Notably, the close alignment between Type II activities and regular curriculum topics may be more important for large groups of students than students pursuing individual investigations.

When students engage in group investigations, they have the opportunity to connect with others who are working on the same learning objectives. While managing group training activities, teachers must offer directions and facilitate student interactions. For teachers who want to provide Type II training activities to their whole class, it would be worthwhile to incorporate intentional learning opportunities for Type II training within the regular curricular unit.

You may also want to consider having materials on hand for individual Type II activities. You may find that some, but not all, of your students are ready to advance their understanding of regular curricular topics. Some students may have already mastered the skills being practiced by the whole class and could benefit from engaging in self-selected activities independently. It may be helpful to reserve materials like puzzles, challenge cards, or virtual workshops to facilitate and differentiate individual student explorations.

As with Type I topics, students should be able to share their preferences and interests for Type II investigations. If you have vetted a variety of materials or strategies to determine their potential for promoting the development of necessary skills, then you can rest assured that a student's choice to engage in one of the self-selected activities will only serve to improve their learning outcomes. Students may be excited and motivated to practice Type II skills, especially when they have been able to pick the activities they complete. A great way to start with creative thinking skills is an activity such as brainstorming or giving students story starters that are creative and fun and asking them to complete the story, either in writing, verbally, or by acting it out.

Type II Enrichment Activities: Evaluation

The beauty of the Enrichment Triad Model can be found in its inherent adaptability to the needs of your classroom. It would be pointless to continue conducting Type II activities if you and your students do not find these activities worthwhile. This is why it is important to reflect on your experience teaching Type II Enrichment. Upon completion of an activity, ask yourself what worked and what did not. Ask your students what worked for them. If applicable, ask another teacher to come in and observe a Type II training in action and describe what they observed. Evaluating the activity in such a way empowers you to keep what worked in your classroom and reconsider how to change the rest.

Conclusion

In this chapter, we have discussed ways to engage and motivate students by focusing on their interests and helping them develop the thinking and planning skills needed to pursue those interests. Research on the Enrichment Triad Model and the SEM Model suggests that these types of talent development opportunities can motivate students to explore high-interest areas and become actively engaged in their learning (Reis and Peters, 2021). In short, high levels of engagement and joyful learning occur when students have the time to develop and pursue their interests, a message we will explore in more depth in the next chapter.

References

Allen, J. K., Robbins, M. A., Payne, Y. D., and Brown, K. B. (2016). Using enrichment clusters to address the needs of culturally and linguistically diverse learners. *Gifted Child Today*, 39(2), 84–97. https://doi.org/10.1177/1076217516628568

Coxon, S., and Cody, R. (2022). The role of STEAM and robotics in developing talent. In J. VanTassel-Baska and C. A. Little (Eds.), *Content-based Curriculum for Advanced Learners* (4th ed., pp. 379–393). Taylor & Francis.

Fiddyment, G. E. (2014). Implementing enrichment clusters in elementary schools: Lessons learned. *Gifted Child Quarterly*, 58(4), 287–296. https://doi.org/10.1177/0016986214547635

González-Pérez, L. I., and Ramírez-Montoya, M. S. (2022). Components of Education 4.0 in 21st century skills frameworks: Systematic review. *Sustainability*, 14(3), 1–31. https://doi.org/10.3390/su14031493

Gubbins, E. J. (1995) *Research Related to the Enrichment Triad Model* (RM95212). University of Connecticut, The National Research Center of the Gifted and Talented. https://nrcgt.uconn.edu/wp-content/uploads/sites/953/2015/04/rm95212.pdf

Kaul, C. R., Johnsen, S. K., Witte, M. M., and Saxon, T. F. (2015). Critical components of a summer enrichment program for urban low-income gifted students. *Gifted Child Today*, 38(1), 32–40. https://eric.ed.gov/?id=EJ1050182

Madaus, J., Cascio, A., Delgado, J., Gelbar, N., Reis, S., and Tarconish, E. (2023). Improving the transition to college for 2e students with ASD: Perspectives from college service providers. *Career Development and Transition for Exceptional Individuals*, 46(1), 40–51. https://doi.org/10.1177/21651434221091230

Madden, M. E., Baxter, M., Beauchamp, H., Bouchard, K., Habermas, D., Huff, M., Ladd, B., Pearon, J., and Plague, G. (2013). Rethinking STEM education: An interdisciplinary STEAM curriculum. *Procedia Computer Science*, 20, 541–546. https://doi.org/10.1016/j.procs.2013.09.316

Plass, J. L., Homer, B. D., and Kinzer, C. K. (2015). Foundations of game-based learning. *Educational Psychologist*, 50(4), 258–283. https://doi.org/10.1080/00461520.2015.1122533

Reis, S. M., Baum, S. M., and Burke, E. (2014). An operational definition of 2e learners: Implications and applications. *Gifted Child Quarterly*, 58(3), 217–230. https://doi.org/10.1177/0016986214534976

Reis, S., Gelbar, N., and Madaus, J. (2022). Pathways to academic success: Specific strength-based teaching and support strategies for twice exceptional high school students with autism spectrum disorder. *Gifted Education International*, 39(3), 378–400. https://doi.org/10.1177/02614294221124197

Reis, S. M., Gentry, M., and Maxfield, L. R. (1998). The application of enrichment clusters to teachers' classroom practices. *Journal for the Education of the Gifted*, 21(3), 310–334. https://doi.org/10.1177/016235329802100304

Reis, S. M., Madaus, J. W., Gelbar, N. W., and Miller, L. J. (2022). Strength-based strategies for 2e high school students with autism spectrum disorder. *TEACHING Exceptional Children*, 21(3), 310–334. https://doi.org/10.1177/016235329802100304

Reis, S. M., McGuire, J. M., and Neu, T. W. (2000). Compensation strategies used by high-ability students with learning disabilities who succeed in college. *Gifted Child Quarterly*, 44(2), 123–134. https://doi.org/10.1177/001698620004400205

Reis, S. M., and Peters, P. M. (2021). Research on the schoolwide enrichment model: Four decades of insights, innovation, and evolution. *Gifted Education International*, 37(2), 109–141. https://doi.org/10.1177/0261429420963987

Reis, S. M., Renzulli, S. J., and Renzulli, J. S. (2021). Enrichment and gifted education pedagogy to develop talents, gifts, and creative productivity. *Education Sciences*, 11(10), 615. https://doi.org/10.3390/educsci11100615

Renzulli, J. S. (1977). The enrichment triad model: A plan for developing defensible programs for the gifted and talented. *Gifted Child Quarterly*, 21(2), 227–233. https://doi.org/10.1177/001698627702100216

Renzulli, J. S. (2012). Reexamining the role of gifted education and talent development for the 21st century: A four-part theoretical approach. *Gifted Child Quarterly*, 56(3), 150–159. https://doi.org/10.1177/0016986212444901

Renzulli, J. S., and Reis, S. M. (1997). *The Schoolwide Enrichment Model: A Comprehensive Plan for Educational Excellence*. Creative Learning Press.

# 5

Implementing Project-Based Learning and Type III Enrichment in Your Classroom

How would you describe your students' engagement in their communities? Over the last few decades, educators of academically gifted and high-potential students have been implementing project-based learning, also known as Type III Enrichment, by asking students to identify problems within their local schools, communities, and states. These activities have inspired students to create solutions to these concerns, encouraging them to consider how they can contribute to the improvement of their communities. Such opportunities are especially appropriate for students identified as 2e, who benefit from thinking about complex challenges in a structured environment.

The goals of Type III Enrichment projects are varied and important. This kind of enrichment involves activities that support students in pursuing a self-selected project, acquiring advanced knowledge, and engaging in process training related to their interests. A core attribute of this type of learning enables students to take on the role of a primary investigator and practice thinking like a professional. By implementing Type III Enrichment, teachers can provide opportunities for students to:

1. Apply interests, creative ideas, and task commitment to a self-selected problem or area of study;
2. Acquire an advanced-level understanding of the content and processes in a particular discipline;
3. Develop authentic products that can have an impact on a target audience;
4. Learn self-directed learning skills in areas like planning, organization, and decision-making;
5. Improve feelings of self-confidence, creative accomplishment, and pride.

Type III activities, often referred to as *investigations, projects, or studies*, give students the opportunity to engage in problem-solving using real-world methods used by professionals in their fields of interest. These are especially important goals for our 2e students who often deal with low self-esteem and confidence (Wang and Neihart, 2015). Students are encouraged to create products or performances to address strong personal issues, problems in their communities, or larger issues, which can range widely based on their individual interests and chosen goals. Students have the opportunity to participate in Type III projects covering a wide variety of studies and topics (Reis and Renzulli, 2022). These investigations can be conducted independently or within an *enrichment cluster* of peers who share the same interests.

Consider how your own educational experiences could have been enriched by the chance to explore your interests and enact positive change in your community. Your students have the potential to create authentic products that can bring about positive change in their communities. It is essential to encourage this goal and give your students opportunities to tackle complex challenges. Research, both current and past, consistently demonstrates that students find Type III projects to be enagaging, beneficial, and relevant to their perceptions of their own identities (Reis and Peters, 2021). Students who complete thoughtful and reflective Type III Investigations not only enhance their own learning but feel inspired to pursue further study. Making meaningful connections with this type of learning can be a powerful motivator, and it should be accessible to all students, regardless of their backgrounds, strengths, or academic achievements.

Type III Project-based Enrichment and Strength-Based Learning

Consider what life might be like for students in your classroom who are required to spend most of their time learning content they have either already mastered or struggle to understand. Although many students will agree that they *should* continue to work on non-engaging content, they may become frustrated or bored when all of their time is spent on tasks that they find uninteresting or impossible. In these scenarios, utilizing the strength-based learning model described in the Schoolwide Enrichment Model (SEM) can be beneficial. Both qualitative and quantitative longitudinal studies on SEM programs have demonstrated positive affective outcomes for students (Reis and Peters, 2021).

It is important for students to increase their skills in areas of challenge, but it is also necessary to enable them to grow in areas of interest. As students mature and gain new skills, they may choose to create projects that allow them to share their interests and talents with others. This is where Type III Investigations come into play! Extensive research on the Enrichment Triad Model demonstrates that Type III Investigations improve students' creative productivity and engagement by facilitating authentic problem-solving opportunities aligned with their personal interests. Pursuing advanced-level activities through independent investigations augments students' desire to learn and encourages them to apply themselves to more focused and enjoyable learning experiences.

Most Type III Investigations produce tangible work that students are able to share with others who have similar interests. For example, a group of students passionate about gardening and landscape architecture might engage in a project to beautify a blighted area of their town. They could share their plans with the local garden club and find volunteers and funding to support their project. The impact of Type III Investigations extends beyond the students and their immediate surroundings. Many of these investigations culminate in service-learning projects, developing unique and unusual products such as websites, videos, pictures, prototypes, school gardens, and clubs, which often have wide-reaching effects.

Participating in enrichment projects helps students gain a deeper understanding of their strengths by allowing them to focus on topics that genuinely interest them. This focus enables them to leverage their knowledge to develop practical solutions that can be beneficial to others. Instead of viewing schools as places to address knowledge acquisition, Type III Investigations can motivate students to see schools as venues for applying their existing knowledge. This transformation can lead to reversing potential underachievement, making schools places where students can learn and grow regardless of their prior experiences.

Type III Enrichment: Where to Start?

Using the SEM, students are encouraged to transform their academic potential into creative productivity. The Enrichment Triad Model can help you implement these types of enrichment experiences in your classroom, and Type III Investigations fit perfectly with the Project-Based Learning approach. These experiences allow students to expand their work beyond K-12 education, offering creative outlets that increase the likelihood of continued engagement in creative endeavors as adults, regardless of their chosen discipline, field of study, or professional trajectory (Reis and Peters, 2021). This benefits students by helping them acquire valuable skills that contribute to their success in both academic and personal settings.

Introducing project-based learning in your classroom helps to prepare your students for their future endeavors and gives them the tools to further their learning while pursuing their unique goals and aspirations. Type III products can be completed by students at any grade level, from pre-kindergarten to high school, in both classrooms and enrichment programs. Here are some project-based enrichment experiences that you could discuss with your students to help inspire similar opportunities in your classroom:

- Create an illustrated book to inform children about a topic of interest (e.g. dinosaurs, castles, concussions);
- Raise funds to support a nonprofit organization that shelters homeless cats;
- Create a blog to inform the community about the importance of various Parks and Recreation services;
- Design a website with tips and tricks for new video game players;
- Create a video about a topic of interest or your favorite underwater animal;
- Teach a class to examine the underrepresentation of women in the field of computer science;
- Create an art gallery to draw attention to various societal issues;
- Create a small company to rebuild and distribute computers to families from lower-income households;
- Develop a solar water heater;
- Organize a community food drive;
- Write a book about chemotherapy from a child's perspective;
- Develop a computer program to help police officers identify areas to increase patrolling.

In the following sections, we provide you with forms and guidelines for getting started on projects in your classroom. We describe how these forms can be used to help students get started and provide examples of successful Type III Investigations that you can share with your students. As you begin, remember that students of all achievement levels, regardless of labels, deserve the opportunity to engage in project-based learning Type III Investigations.

The Action Information Form

You may be well aware of the topics and subjects that are of particular interest to the students in your classroom. However, you might feel pressured to wait to enable your 2e students to explore their interests through projects until they show improved performance across academic areas. As we have discussed, while some students already have a strong interest in certain areas, they may experience learning challenges in other subjects. For example, you may have a student who has difficulty with decoding and asks to work on a project related to video games instead of silent reading. It is important to remember that students can actually improve their deficit areas by working on areas of interest. You could, for example, encourage your student to play a reading video game or have them gamify a specific skill.

As you know, when students are not appropriately challenged, they may begin to underachieve in school. However, these same students will demonstrate high levels of focus and attention when working in areas of interest. Research discussed earlier in this book has shown that programs focusing on the strengths and talents of 2e students can improve educational outcomes, foster a positive attitude toward school, and boost self-confidence.

Facilitating Student Discussion

Depending on the grade level that you teach, you may find it helpful to use the simple Lightbulb Form included in Appendix F. The lightbulb *Action Information Messages* form highlights the importance of interest in promoting students' academic enjoyment and motivation. Students can provide information about their general subject area of interest, their specific idea for a project, or a description of possible directions and resources needed as they begin their Type III Investigation. *The Action Information Messages* form was developed to facilitate discussions with students who are in the early stages of their Type III projects. You might start this process by engaging your student individually or you could involve other educators, including those from different content areas or special education. A flexible approach can be particularly beneficial for working with 2e students who express different strengths with different adults. Other teachers may have noticed specific details about your students' skills, background, or interests that may be of helpful to you. They might also have strategies or conversation starters that they use to help students explore their interests. These discussions may help you to understand a little more about how your students perceive themselves within the context of their interests. Additionally, speaking with your students' parents can provide valuable insights into their interests and hobbies outside of the classroom.

Another process that may help you is to consider if your student is willing and able to start a project are discussions about readiness. To make that decision, you can initiate a discussion with the student and consider the following: is this project in the students' area of personal interest? How long has your student had an interest in this area? Is the student excited abut this work? What kinds of assistance will they need? Will your student be able to expend the time and focus to complete this project? Conversations with your students may come naturally to students as they may be excited to share their thoughts and ideas with you. These worksheets can be particularly helpful when you initiate a conversation with new, quiet, or shy students.

When you have these discussions with your students, try to ask questions that will help you dive deeper. Ask questions that are open-ended. Asking 'what,' 'why,' and 'how' questions will give you far more information than closed-ended questions that only require 'yes' or 'no' responses. For example, you may ask your students to reflect on the following questions:

- ◆ What topic are you interested in?
- ◆ Why are you interested in this topic?
- ◆ How long have you been interested in this topic?
- ◆ Is there anyone else in your life who is also interested in this topic?

- Have you contacted anyone to learn more about this topic?
- Have you ever tried to engage in a project related to this topic? Why or why not?
- In your own words, what would you say that experts in this topic do? If you were an expert in this area, what kind of work would you do?
- Are you willing to spend time on this work every day?

By asking questions like the ones above, you enable your students to share their experiences and demonstrate their level of interest and commitment to a particular topic. You may find that a student expresses interest in a topic because their parents are interested in it or because it aligns with the interests of a particular social group. This information will help identify whether a Type III Investigation about the topic will be appropriate and useful.

To gauge your students' interest and dedication to a topic, ask them to discuss the steps they believe should come next. Knowing the procedures required to pursue their interests can be indicative of their commitment to potential projects in that area. They may already have interest-related goals that you can use to craft their Type III Investigation. The following questions will help you decipher a student's task commitment to a specific area of interest:

- How do you think you should get started?
- How many hours do you believe it will take you to complete the next step?
- How many other students will need to be involved?
- Who else do you need to talk to and how will you contact them?
- What information do you think experts in your field collect? How do you think you could gather this information?
- How do you think you could use your interest to solve a problem or create something

Make sure to pay attention to students' responses to determine if they are genuinely willing to put in the effort to complete a service or product. During these conversations, students may realize that they are not as interested in taking the necessary steps as they initially thought. These questions will actualize the concept of interest, which will help them figure out for themselves what they want. If they truly see themselves as experts in the field of interest they have described, they will be invigorated, rather than intimidated, by this discussion and will be ready to take the next steps in a Type III Investigation. Remember that students who are not ready for a Type III Investigation in one interest area might be ready in another. Be attentive to behaviors that may indicate alternative interests.

Planning Appropriate Projects and Type III Investigations

When your discussion successfully demonstrates a student's realistic and high level of interest in a project, your next step is to determine what the finished product will look like, when and where the work will take place, the steps needed, and the types of support and resources. Recording these details will help clarify your student's project's intended objective and ensure that the students' goals are being met within a reasonable timeframe. Using an adaptation of the *Management Plan for Individual and Small Group Investigations* (see Appendix G) can help you and your students identify objectives, resources, and potential outlets and audiences for the creative products they develop. In many ways, this step also facilitates the development of students' executive function skills. Engaging in a long-term project enhances the ability to sustain attention, focus on goals, resist distractions, and learn from past experiences.

Often, an academic exploration begins by carefully analyzing and synthesizing pre-existing information, but the investigation does not end there. A major goal of project-based enrichment is to create something new with the researched information. This involves helping students grow their comprehension beyond merely summarizing what they already know. The results of a Type III Investigation should be a creative accomplishment that is useful and relevant to the selected audience, and never a standard type of school report. Students should come away from this experience aware of how their efforts have positively transformed their field of interest. It is important to note that many students do not understand the wide range of products or services that they can provide. Your role as a teacher is to offer students different ways to creatively express the information they are learning.

Type III Enrichment: Researching Like an Expert

In order to understand which creative endeavors would lead to positive change, you should encourage students to look at what experts in the field know about their subject. Ask your students to take on the perspective of an expert. Prompt your students to consider what professional minds have to say about what is already known, the techniques used to gather and report the information, and what questions future researchers should explore. You do not necessarily need to know what these questions are, as they will vary greatly between fields of study. However, you should be ready to guide your students to resources that contain this information.

A classic book entitled *Understanding History: A Primer of Historical Method* (Gottschalk, 1953) serves as an example of the type of questions to guide Type III Investigations. In this resource, the authors included a list of questions that historians can use to help them as they engage in *problem-finding* and *focusing*. These types of questions are provided below:

1. **Geographical Questions.** Geographical questions center around the interrogative (*Where?*). What areas of the world do I wish to investigate?
2. **Biographical Questions.** Biographical questions center around the interrogative (*Who?*). What persons am I interested in researching?

3. **Chronological Questions.** Chronological questions center around the interrogative (*When?*). What period of the past do I wish to study?
4. **Occupational Questions.** Occupational Questions center around the interrogative (*What?*). What spheres of human interest concern me the most? What kinds of human activity?

Although these questions are framed with junior historians in mind, they can prompt students interested in various content areas. For example, students interested in studying biospheres may respond very differently to the geographical prompt, with some opting to study the Amazon Rainforest and others choosing to examine the Great Barrier Reef. Alternatively, students who are interested in exploring physics and music may be particularly drawn to biographical prompts, idealizing experts like Stephen Hawking or Louis Armstrong.

What if your students can't find enough information? Encourage them to view information gaps from several different perspectives. Ask them to consider what is unknown about a subject and what factors may have influenced the current lack of knowledge. This approach activates their critical thinking skills and provides a strong foundation for their work. Students should consider how individual characteristics and societal expectations might influence the way they approach a research topic. For example, researchers have noted that female scientists often ask different questions than their male counterparts, leading to a deeper understanding of the subject (Roy, 2008). Additionally, people from diverse cultural backgrounds contribute uniquely to various scientific fields (Pomeroy, 1994). Students should not feel pressured to separate different facets of their identity in their academic pursuits. Instead, teachers should encourage them to draw from their unique cultural and personal backgrounds as they generate questions that could deepen their understanding of their areas of interest. For 2e students, these can be particularly meaningful opportunities to explore their strengths.

Raw Data

While you support your students in moving beyond writing traditional reports to developing authentic Type III products, it can be helpful to discuss the concept of raw data. Raw data includes all types of unorganized bits of information that researchers gather. As researchers analyze these pieces of information, they organize them in ways that support an argument, reach a conclusion, discover a principle, or create a unique product or presentation.

Consider the difference between a book report and a fully fleshed-out persuasive essay about character perspectives. In a book report, students summarize key plots without analyzing the information in the text, which is highly structured and mechanical. In contrast, writing a persuasive essay about character perspectives requires a deeper understanding of the source material and careful selection of information. For this type of product, students would include quotes from selected characters and produce high-quality essays with potentially different conclusions. This approach illustrates how students can collect and use data. Understanding how and why your students will use the information they gather is crucial in pursuing a Type III Investigation.

It should be noted that teachers do not have to be experts in every field. Instead, your job is to help your students engage in problem-focusing and problem-solving. It often helps to focus on developing a support system for your students as they participate in project-based Type III Enrichment activities. This could involve directing students to methodological resources, obtaining informational resources they might not access otherwise, and offering scaffolding tips.

Remember that you also have resources that are available to you as a teacher. There are hundreds of online resources that can provide you with tips and educational materials as your students begin their Type III. These include:

- Discovery Education (www.discoveryeducation.com)
- PBS Learning Media (https://cptv.pbslearningmedia.org)

- Smithsonian Learning Lab (https://learninglab.si.edu)
- The Teacher's Corner (www.theteacherscorner.net/librarians/)

Consider using the mentioned resources to help your students get started on their research. You may want to suggest to your students that they ask school or local librarians and other professionals within various fields for advice about finding resource materials that can be helpful. The Teacher's Corner offers links to resources that can be useful to librarians and teachers as they assist students in collecting educational resources. Communicate to your students that they may need to look beyond the usual school resources to find specialized materials and resource persons, even if appropriate educational materials are available at school. At this stage in their research, students may need your help speaking with various professionals, accessing educational materials, or brainstorming ideas. The support you provide during this stage will be invaluable to their success!

The Editorial and Feedback Process

Receiving criticism about one's work, even if it is constructive, can be challenging for students who are beginning a new type of work. For those learning about a field that they are passionate about, feedback about how to improve can be especially difficult to hear and accept. Students should understand that even the most experienced researchers, writers, and creative producers must continuously reflect on their work. To help your students reach the highest level of excellence, provide constructive feedback in a way that is encouraging. Your students should view your feedback as motivating, as you provide positive, sensitive, and specific recommendations for ways to improve their work.

One effective way to sensitively promote high-quality work is to show your students outstanding examples of products created by others, especially if these examples are completed by students of the same age or those pursuing similar areas of study. By examining the work of others, students can reflect on how to improve their own work. Rather than you saying, 'This is what your work is missing,' students can compare their own work with that of another student and say, 'This is what I might be missing' or 'This is what I can do to make my project better.' Such reflective exercises help students identify potential areas of growth and specific solutions to address these concerns. You may want to display a poem like this in your classroom to reinforce the idea that even excellent work can be improved:

> *Good better best,*
> *Never let it rest,*
> *Until the good is better,*
> *Until the better is best*
>
> *(St. Jerome prayers)*

Finding the Right Target Audience

As you may have guessed, Type III projects and studies offer students the opportunity to engage in *authentic learning*. As described by Joseph Renzulli, authentic learning involves the application of relevant knowledge, critical thinking skills, and interpersonal skills to solve real-world problems. Real-life problems are inherently directed toward an authentic audience with a genuine interest in the service being presented by the student. Renzulli provides an example of a Type III Investigation, discussing how students presented their findings to two different audiences: a 'contrived' audience (classmates helping rehearse presentation skills) and a real audience (members of a local historical society, veterans' groups, the families of servicemen, and participants of a local event commemorating Vietnam veterans). He found that students did better and felt more accomplished when presenting to a real audience over a fake one.

Given that Type III Investigations center around real-life problems, it is important for students to identify a real audience who will benefit from the presentation of the project. A focus on real audiences and outlets is perhaps one of the most exciting aspects of Type III Investigations. Through interacting with real audiences during the development and presentation of Type III projects, students can learn how their efforts may help to change the actions, attitudes, and beliefs of others. Facilitators of this type of project-based learning have found that providing students with a sense of gravity motivates them to improve the quality of their products. Producing a quality Type III Investigation will guide students toward appropriate means of disseminating results to interested parties.

Understanding who students wish to share their Type III projects with helps them understand why they wish to do this project Therefore, it is important to discuss real audiences early in the planning process of a Type III Investigation. Students may easily identify someone they know who would be an authentic audience member interested in their project, which might even be the reason for their interest in the topic.

When students struggle to identify viable audiences, they can benefit from concrete examples. Consultating relevant how-to books and interacting with professionals in the student's area of interest can provide valuable insights for brainstorming potential audience groups. Additionally, we have included a list of potential opportunities for students, titled *Vehicles and Products for Type III Investigations* (Figure 5.1). This resource provides several opportunities for authentic presentation, categorized by interest area.

Independent and Small Group Projects

It is important to remember that project-based learning, especially independent studyprojects, will be new for some of your students. Therefore, it's natural for them to have many questions about how independent projects work. Figure 5.2 provides further information about independent projects. While students typically follow these steps when completing independent or small group studies or projects, they may sometimes accomplish these steps in a non-sequential order.

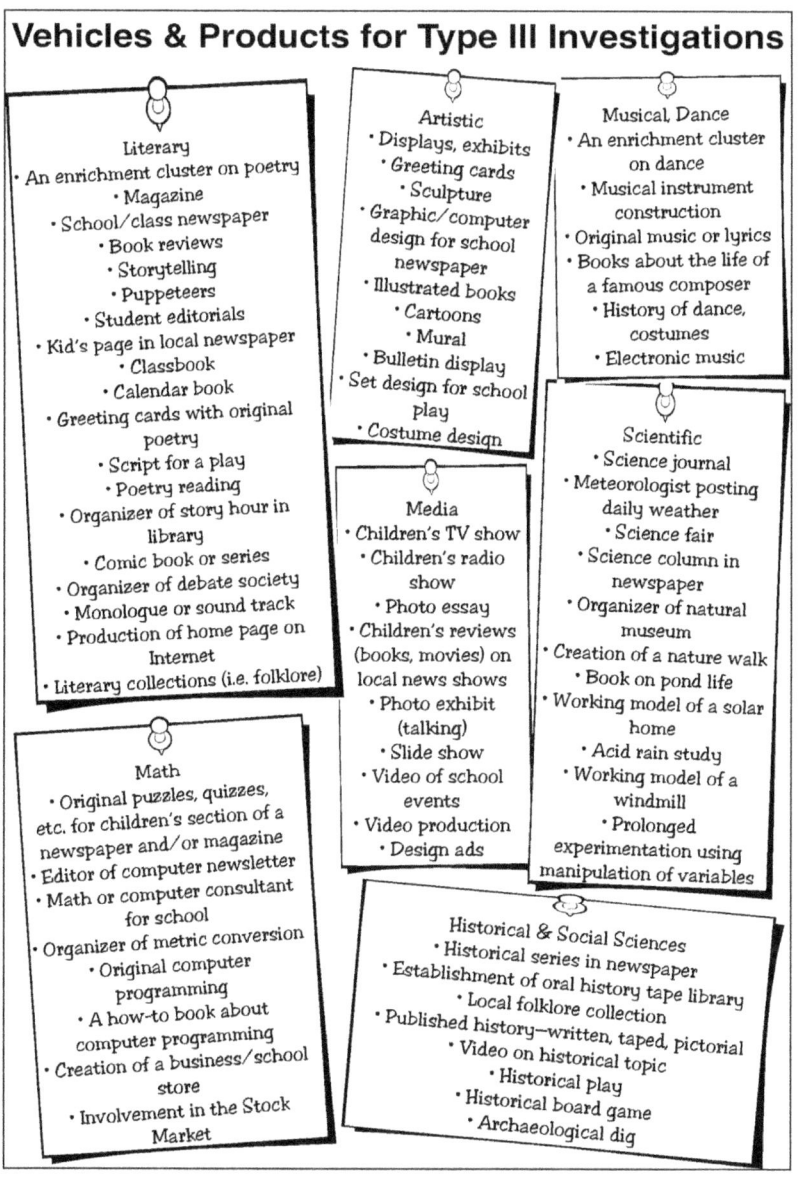

FIGURE 5.1 Vehicles and Products for Type III Investigations

Many project ideas vary depending on the specific interests of students. For example, the Renzulli Learning website's Wizard Project Maker includes independent projects called Super Starter Projects, which you can use to help your students produce

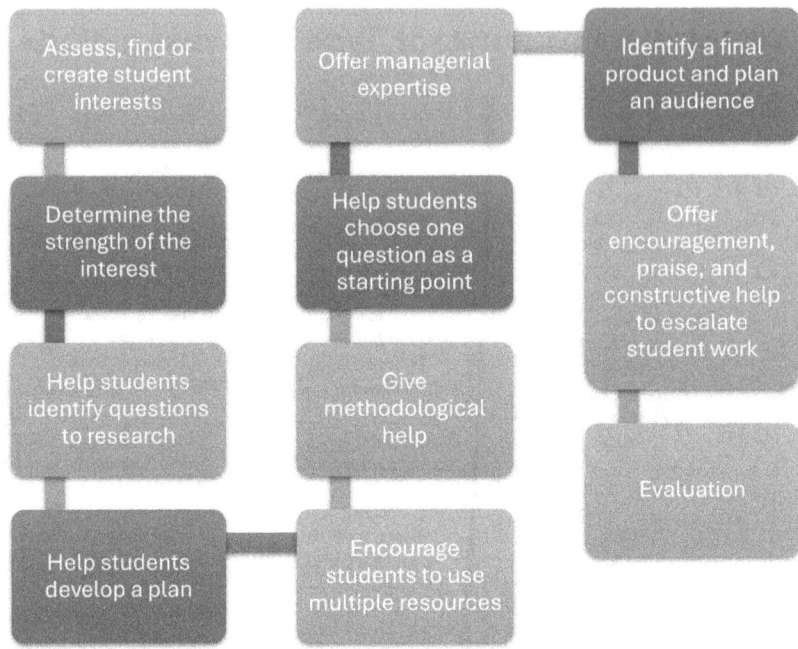

FIGURE 5.2 Steps for Guiding Students through Independent and Self-Selected Projects

high-quality enrichment projects (see Figure 5.3 for examples). Super Starter Projects provide how-to resources, suggestions for creative work, and activities that will help your students think like independent researchers.

Evaluation

The final stage of any independent, self-selected project is evaluation. It is important to provide meaningful, constructive feedback to help students reflect on their efforts with purpose. You may need to provide scaffolding support as students learn to critique their own work constructively. Students should assess their own work by answering the following questions:

1. What did you enjoy about working on your project?
2. What were the greatest challenges or obstacles, and how did you address them?

Castle Builder
http://score.rims.k12.ca.us/activity/castle_builder/

- You are a Medieval Castle Builder living in Wales in the year 1076. You are hired by the Norman Baron William de Clare to build him a fantastic castle in Aberystwyth, Wales. This site houses an activity that will help you get started building your own historically accurate castle!

Why Do Civilizations Fall Apart?
http://www.learner.org/exhibits/collapse/

- Find out more about what caused famous civiliazations to fall apart using this interactive site. Examine the clues left at archeological sites to learn more about four civilizations. Record your findings in a journal and check

Building Tools to Watch the Weather
http://www.fi.edu/weather/todo/todo.html

- Use the tools on this website to make your own weather station. Build your own barometer, compass, rain gauge, and thermometer using the links on the page. All the materials and instructions are listed!

FIGURE 5.3 Examples of Super Starter Projects

3. What did you learn while completing your project?
4. Were you satisfied with the final product? If so, in what ways?
5. What could you have done to improve your final project?
6. Who or what helped you with your project?
7. What resources supported you the most?
8. Do you think you might like to do a similar project in the future?
9. Do you have any ideas for your next project?

Exercises to Enhance Critical and Evaluative Thinking

When facilitating independent student learning, it's essential to employ metacognitive strategies that involve thought articulation and evaluation. For example, a teacher might solve a math problem on the board while verbally explaining each step and explicitly stating the reasoning behind each decision. This could involve saying out loud, 'Why did I choose this method?' or 'What would happen if I tried another approach?' This kind of verbalization helps students understand both the 'how' and the 'why' behind problem-solving strategies. By navigating these critical thinking processes, students will be better equipped to succeed in their current and future educational activities. Consider asking your students open-ended questions and encouraging them to use self-assessments. We have previously provided several questions for use during learning projects, but it is important to give opportunities for practicing self-assessment before and after learning activities as well.

For example, you may help your students learn how to evaluate online resources. Identifying the helpful and unhelpful features of instructional websites can be challenging for students. You may need to model evaluation criteria through various discussion prompts. This is a critical skill for students as they learn to use resource descriptions to evaluate the value of information. To develop this understanding, spend time reviewing specific websites with your students and discussing their features. You should view these discussions as opportunities to model and demonstrate decision-making skills. And remember that websites may have both helpful features, like accessible and informative content, and unhelpful features, such as confusing graphics or phrasing. Encouraging students to evaluate resources this way will improve their abilities as independent learners.

You may wonder why evaluation skills are so important. In 1998, Lyle Zapato created a fictional endangered species known as the tree octopus, which allegedly could live both on land and in the sea. Educational researchers, including Don Leu of the University of Connecticut, used the fake website to understand how many students fell for false information. The findings revealed that students were largely resistant to changing their beliefs even when presented with evidence debunking the existence of the Pacific Northwest Tree Octopus. This highlights the prevalence and impact of false information on the internet. Visit the site yourself to see the importance of gathering additional evidence and using critical thinking to verify the legitimacy of information: [Tree Octopus] (https://zapatopi.net/treeoctopus/).

Consider using the following discussion prompts to help strengthen students' critical thinking processes:

1. Can you read and understand this resource?
2. What type of site is this (e.g., a game site, an information site, a skill site, a site that lets you create something, etc.)?
3. Are the graphics clear and understandable?
4. Does this site have the type of information you expected? Is anything suspicious about it?
5. Can you find at least two other sites that support the information you read on this site?
6. Is this resource something that will help you learn more about your topic?
7. Does this resource teach you something new or help you practice something you already know?
8. Can you create a product (some type of work) on this site that you can share with others?

If your students need extra support in understanding the dangers of false information, consider facilitating a classroom discussion where students take turns presenting their critiques of a given resource. Activities like these can broaden students' perspectives and teach them to be critical consumers of online information.

Type III Enrichment: Examples of Successful Investigations

Over the course of four decades, SEM efforts, particularly Type III projects, have brought about positive, meaningful, and lasting changes to different communities and fields of study worldwide. When students complete a successful Type III project, they gain a broader understanding of the impact of their efforts that extends beyond the scope of their classroom. This has been evidenced by numerous students who participated in Type III Investigations over time. Reis and Renzulli (2022) documented several Type III projects that have improved society and promoted service and social responsibility. For example, high school students participating in a Type III project were determined to establish a bike path in a local city. They actively engaged local politicians to address legal policies and financial issues, demonstrating their commitment to the cause. Their dedication paid off when their dreams were realized and the bike path was successfully built. Further examples of these projects discussed by Reis and Renzulli (2022) are provided below, completed by students of various achievement levels, including 2e.

Jacob
Four years prior to the beginning of his official Type III project, Jacob began to notice a significant income disparity between local families who had computers and families who did not. From his observation, he determined that families who earn a high income are more likely to have reliable access to a computer as compared to families with a low income. When he and his friends were just nine years old, they decided to create a company called 'Computers for Communities, Inc.' Through this project, Jacob was able to rebuild and distribute over 1,000 computers to families from lower-income households.

Xóchitl
At the time of her Type III Investigation, Xóchitl was an eight-year-old girl living in Mexico. In her community, it was common to heat water by burning firewood from cut logs. However, due to the environmental hazards and implications of this practice, residents often refrained from taking hot showers. In response, Xóchitl developed a solar water heater that her community members could use to take hot baths or showers. To ensure that others could benefit from her work, Xóchitl chose not to patent her product, thereby increasing access to safe and hygienic cleaning systems for neighboring towns.

William
William was an eight-year-old boy living in Raleigh, North Carolina, who decided to research BackPack Buddies, an interfaith food Shuttle

program. This innovative hunger relief organization served seven counties in North Carolina with a goal of providing healthy meals on the weekends for students from low-income households. After speaking with a representative from the organization, William decided to set up a food drive with his school community to collect food for the program. Over the course of a month, he collected more than a thousand pounds of food, which were donated to local families in need. Following his initial project, William made plans to expand this contribution in the future with the goal of starting a state-wide food drive.

Naudia

When Naudia was in the third grade, she learned that her friend had been diagnosed with cancer. She had many pressing questions about the diagnosis, such as the type of medicine her friend would need, the likelihood of the treatment's success, and the effects of chemotherapy. Unfortunately, not many people are prepared to answer the multitude of questions that she posed about this emotionally challenging topic. Naudia began a mission to assist her friend in overcoming cancer and to provide support to other children in similar circumstances. To find the answers to her questions, Naudia wrote a book about her friend's journey called 'My Friend Linkin.' This book describes a typical day of chemotherapy treatment from a child's perspective. Over time, **My Friend Linkin** *has evolved into a book series and nonprofit organization committed to raising awareness about childhood cancers. Through this organization, children whose lives have been affected by cancer can share their stories and motivate others to make a difference.*

Jeremy

When Jeremy was in fifth grade, his uncle tragically lost his life in an incident involving a drunk driver. In response, Jeremy took decisive action by organizing a chapter of Students Against Driving Drunk at his elementary and local middle schools. However, Jeremy wanted to delve deeper into the factors leading up to the incident. Although his family provided information about the driver and the circumstances, Jeremy sought to understand the consequences for those who overserved their customers. Determined to investigate, Jeremy decided to write a computer program to analyze police data on the location and frequency of arrests and accidents related to drunk driving. Although his initial request for data was dismissed by the police, Jeremy's persistence paid off when he submitted a proposal to the Board of Safety and was granted access to the information. Over several months, he developed a computer program to analyze the intersections between arrests and accidents. As a result, he was able to identify areas where bar staff may have been overserving, prompting an increased police presence and leading to more drunk driving arrests. Despite the long and arduous journey, Jeremy's efforts made a significant impact on the community, honoring his uncle's memory.

Type III: Keeping Students Engaged and Motivated

Integrating the Enrichment Triad Model and Type III Investigations to offer enrichment opportunities can yield numerous benefits that extend far beyond the typical classroom experience. These benefits include the progress of student's efforts toward a larger goal. This exemplifies the overarching goal of Type III Enrichment: to help students begin to think, feel, and act like creative producers.

Through their active participation in Type III Investigation experiences, your students will begin to see themselves as capable researchers and scholars. They will recognize their own potential to act as active agents in the fields that draw their inspiration. Once they have begun to identify their own strengths, it will be impossible for them to go back to the deficit-based thinking that may have previously characterized their educational experiences.

Increased Motivation and Engagement

The Enrichment Triad Model is designed to be intrinsically motivating for 2e students, as it enables them to choose what interests they want to explore and what products they would like to produce. Joe Renzulli has discussed how activities found in the Enrichment Triad Model can serve as a catalyst for both curiosity and internal motivation (Renzulli, 2012, p. 155). It is understandable that students are motivated to work and study harder because of participation in enrichment opportunities, especially for students coming from lower-income backgrounds who, through enrichment programs, are made aware of new domains of interest.

The outcomes of Type III Investigations extend beyond the achievements students can attain during their projects. Research has found that students engaged in Type III Investigations consider their projects interesting, beneficial, and self-sustaining. The enduring impact of these programs is highlighted in a summary article by Reis and Peters (2021), which discusses the numerous benefits of enrichment. This article argues that students in enrichment programs experience positive socioemotional outcomes. Additionally, the research demonstrates how enrichment programs enhance students' motivation, showing the significant progress students can make not only in their current academic endeavors but also in their post-K-12 experiences.

Maintaining Momentum Beyond Areas of Interest

You may be wondering if students' engagement in their Type III projects will generalize to other academic areas. Remember that Type III projects provide students with the opportunity to complete in-depth enrichment activities. Through the process of completing Type III Investigations, students engage in creative productivity and experience the joys, challenges, and intensities that accompany these creative opportunities. This helps broaden students' awareness of the importance of their education in relation to their creative goals.

When your students find value in the work that they are asked to do, they are demonstrating a high level of a concept called *goal valuation*. Goal valuation refers to the process of assessing and determining the worth or importance of a specific goal. In research exploring students' perceptions of enrichment activities and goal valuation, Brigandi and colleagues (2016) found that students with high goal valuation had more positive attitudes about school and enjoyed completing academic tasks. The researchers explained 'when students are interested in what they are learning and view the outcome of learning is beneficial, they are more likely to learn and more likely to perceive learning as enjoyable' (p. 283). Other studies have shown that students who had completed Type III projects in both elementary and secondary school settings maintained their interests and dispositions toward creative productivity after participating in these investigations (Reis and Peters, 2021). When they use the Enrichment Triad Model, students not only develop creative products but also learn to broaden their thinking and cognitive skills (Surya and Nurdin, 2021). Further, Westberg and Leppien (2018) found that students who completed self-selected investigations in elementary school were more likely to pursue challenges and continue their education into adulthood. The long-term benefits of Type III Investigations cannot be overstated.

These studies summarize the lasting power of Type III Investigations. Too often, students are not given the opportunity to pursue their interests or engage in activities that truly inspire them. They are made to feel as though their unique passions are not important enough to warrant academic exploration. Students deserve time to engage in activities that promote a strength-based, rather than deficit-based, perspective (Reis and Peters, 2021).

Conclusion

Through the project-based learning component in the SEM, you can show your 2e students that you not only acknowledge their individualized interests but are willing to help them cultivate any necessary skills. The question is not *if* enrichment activities like the ones demonstrated in the Enrichment Triad Model are right for your students. The question is *which* activities are right for your students. It is not a matter of whether your students should be given time to pursue research in self-selected areas of interest, but what this research will entail and how you can help them. As you begin to implement the Enrichment Triad Model, you will better understand your students' strengths and interests. You will also be able to recognize how all students, especially those students identified as 2e, are budding creative individuals who, with your support and help, will learn about their own strengths and interests, become young creative producers, and shape their respective communities and fields for generations to come.

References

Brigandi, C. B., Siegle, D., Weiner, J. M., Gubbins, E. J., and Little, C. A. (2016). Gifted secondary school students: The perceived relationship between enrichment and goal valuation. *Journal for the Education of the Gifted*, 39(4), 263–287. https://doi.org/10.1177/0162353216671837

Gottschalk, L. R. (1953). Understanding history: A primer of historical method. *Nursing Research*, 2(1), 44.

Pomeroy, D. (1994). Science education and cultural diversity: Mapping the field. *Studies in Science Education*, 24(1), 49–73. https://doi.org/10.1080/03057269408560039

Reis, S. M., and Peters, P. M. (2021). Research on the schoolwide enrichment model: Four decades of insights, innovation, and evolution. *Gifted Education International*, 37(2), 109–141. https://doi.org/10.1177/0261429420963987

Reis, S. M., and Renzulli, J. S. (2022). Transformational giftedness: Using SEM pedagogy to create future leaders and change agents dedicated to service, social responsibility, and using their talents to improve the planet. In R. J. Sternberg, D. Ambrose, and S. Karami (Eds.), *The Palgrave Handbook of Transformational Giftedness for Education* (pp. 313–333). Springer International Publishing.

Renzulli, J. S. (2012). Reexamining the role of gifted education and talent development for the 21st century: A four-part theoretical approach. *Gifted Child Quarterly*, 56(3), 150–159. https://doi.org/10.1177/0016986212444901

Roy, D. (2008). Asking different questions: Feminist practices for the natural sciences. *Hypatia*, 23(4), 134–157. https://doi.org/10.1111/j.1527-2001.2008.tb01437.x

Surya, R. A., and Nurdin, E. A. (2021). Utilizing the enrichment triad model in history learning: A conceptual framework. *Paramita: Historical Studies Journal*, 31(1), 139–147. http://dx.doi.org/10.15294/paramita.v31i1.26717

Wang, C. W., and Neihart, M. (2015). Academic self-concept and academic self-efficacy: Self-beliefs enable academic achievement of 2e students. *Roeper Review*, 37(2), 63–73. https://doi.org/10.1080/02783193.2015.1008660

Westberg, K. L., and Leppien, J. H. (2018). Student independent investigations for authentic learning. *Gifted Child Today*, 41(1), 13–18. https://doi.org/10.1177/1076217517735354

Zapato. (2012). *Web Archive Save the Pacific Northwest Tree Octopus*. Library of Congress. www.loc.gov/item/lcwaN0010826

6

All About College

The pursuit of higher education is a pivotal consideration for many 2e students who aspire to leverage their distinct capabilities and actualize their academic and personal goals. Many 2e students hope and plan to go to college. According to a recent study by Madaus et al. (2022), successful 2eASD students indicated that higher education allowed them to engage with their interests and develop their independence and autonomy. Attending college also offers these students important economic benefits. Carnevale, Cheah, and Wenzinger (2021) found that people earn more with each level of college completed, with those holding graduate degrees earning more than those with bachelor's degrees. Similarly, data from the U.S. Bureau of Labor Statistics (2024) shows higher employment rates for Americans with disabilities who attended college. These studies highlight the importance of considering a college education for high-potential individuals with disabilities.

Many students with 2e face difficulties in pursuing higher education due to various factors. These include the difficulties in academic and social experiences that they face in high school and college, which can overwhelm their potential. 2e students are often required to meet additional criteria for success as they are asked to alter their neurodiverse brain to fit a neurotypical society. This can lead to frustration, burnout, and feelings of

DOI: 10.4324/9781003511861-6

inadequacy. Without proper support, many 2e students find it challenging to meet the academic and social demands required to achieve a college-level degree.

Many teachers want to help 2e students transition to college but feel unprepared to do so. The significant differences in types and levels of available support exacerbate the challenges associated with the transition to college. This disconnect is demonstrated by the lower rates at which students with disabilities enroll in and complete university programs (Newman et al., 2011; Shattuck et al., 2012). While you may believe that your 2e students have the potential to excel in a college environment, not all 2e individuals in your classroom may have the ability or desire to attend a 4-year university. This decision must be made by the student in collaboration with their families, based on their needs and goals. The advice provided in this chapter is specifically designed for 2e students who want to attend college or university. It is important to note that many of the students we have worked with started their careers at community colleges before transitioning to competitive four-year universities. Keeping an open mind about the future of your 2e students will demonstrate your confidence in their autonomy and personal abilities.

The following chapter describes the experiences of 2e students as they transition to college and offers suggestions to help guide their journey. To do this, we use various section headings that resemble questions your students might be asking themselves as they prepare to transition to college. We will begin this chapter with a quick true/false quiz (see Table 6.1) related to services for students with disabilities in postsecondary education (modified from Merchant and Dintino, 2011). This exercise is useful for students and can be extremely helpful for parents, guardians, and transition professionals. Consider how your students might answer the following questions.

We will revisit this quiz at the end of the chapter. Don't worry about the correct answers; instead, consider how this experience felt for you, and keep in mind any questions you have while reading.

Table 6.1 College Services Quiz

1. The accommodations and modifications in my IEP goals or my Section 504 plan will be continued when I go to college.	T F
2. I will receive modifications to lessons, assignments, tests, and deadlines when I am in college because of my disability.	T F
3. My college disability services office will contact me regularly once I am on campus.	T F
4. My college disability services office will automatically set up the accommodations and services that I need for me.	T F
5. I will be responsible for notifying my professors of my disability if I want to receive accommodations in their class.	T F
6. I may or may not receive the same services in college that I received in high school.	T F
7. I do not have to tell anyone about my disability if I don't want to when I'm in college.	T F
8. When I disclose my disability to the college disability service office, I will automatically receive each accommodation that I request.	T F
9. It doesn't matter when I disclose my disability to my college disability service office.	T F
10. My parents will be able to contact my professors and will be involved in decisions about my coursework.	T F

Why (or Why Not) College?

Before we begin a step-by-step examination of the process of transitioning and applying to colleges for 2e students, it is important to consider why students would want to go to college. One reason is financial. As stated above, students who graduate from college with a four-year degree earn more than those with a high school diploma (Broady and Hershbein, 2020). However, financial considerations extend beyond future earnings. Your students' options for education at the postsecondary level will likely be impacted by their family's current financial status. Encourage your students to think about the cost of university and inform them about available financial aid. Together, you and your students can investigate specific scholarships that may be offered for 2e and disabled individuals.

In addition to financial gains, academically gifted 2e college students have identified three key aspects of college that they found most beneficial (Austermann et al., 2023). First, they enjoyed being able to learn about areas of interest in depth. They appreciated the ability to focus more on areas of interest and explore new topics by taking courses. Second, they enjoyed being around others who loved to learn. Specifically, they noted that they appreciated being in highly specified classes with individuals who share their interests and passions. Third, these 2e students relished the opportunity to gain independence. They indicated that they valued the chance to learn from their mistakes and take ownership of their learning.

Significant Differences Between High School and College

Once your students have expressed an interest in pursuing postsecondary education, it is important to provide them with guidance on the transition from high school to university. College is an exciting time for young adults, as it presents them with the opportunity to learn new things and explore their identities. It can also be a way to meet new people, live in new areas, and experience an independent life away from home. Academically, there are notable distinctions between high school and college that necessitate heightened independence, improved time management skills, and increased levels of self-determination among students. Those who transition to college will notice a change in the structure and nature of academic demands, including course load, meeting times, structure, and grading. Each can impact a student's executive functioning skills, which we discuss later in the chapter. It is helpful to understand these worries as your students enter a new phase of life. Below, we list some of the questions your students may have as they prepare for college.

How Many Courses Should a 2e Student Take in College? An important difference exists between high school and college credit loads, as the number of courses a student might take each semester can vary. Depending on how often and for how long a course meets, it can hold one, two, or three credits at most colleges (note that some colleges follow a slightly different structure). Often, three-credit courses meet two to three times per week for 50- to 75-minute sessions. Some courses in the sciences, psychology, or the arts may also include a 'lab' or 'discussion' requirement that adds another credit and additional time commitments. Many full-time students enroll in 15 to 17 credits per semester, whereas part-time students typically take fewer than 12 credits per semester (Merchant and Dintino, 2011). This means full-time students will take between four and six classes, spending roughly 45 hours per week attending classes and completing coursework. Given that funding can vary depending on students' course loads, it is important for your students to be aware of how many courses they plan on taking and why. Some scholarships may require students to maintain a full-time course load, while others may ask students to work while attending school. Before enrolling in college, students should understand the benefits of being a full- or part-time student.

When Do Courses Meet? Courses might be offered at different times throughout the day, from early morning to late evening. This can create gaps within a daily schedule, making it important for students to use this time wisely. For example, some students could use this gap time to exercise, work, or study. If the student lives on campus, they could go back to their room and sleep or play video games. The choice is up to them, and it is imperative that teachers, parents, and transition specialists support students as they learn to manage their time effectively.

How Are Courses Structured? Just as courses can have different credit loads, they can also have different structures. For example, some courses may be held in large lecture halls with hundreds of students. In these cases, professors tend to give lectures while students are expected to listen and take notes. There is often little interaction between the student and the professor in these types of classes. There are seldom any checks to see if a student is keeping up with assigned readings. Attendance is usually not taken, leaving it up to the students to decide if they will attend and, if they do, what they will do during class. For some students, this may involve listening and taking notes, while others may choose to go online instead. Your students should be prepared to observe both behaviors in class and will likely need guidance on how to listen attentively to lectures while others are distracted.

Other classes might be smaller (think seminar or discussion classes) and may require more interaction with professors or other students. It is important for students to be prepared for discussions and group activities. Other courses still might be set up as labs where students will be provided a set of activities that they need to complete alone or in groups. Your 2e student may prefer these courses as they can engage directly with challenging material and conversation. Alternatively, they might struggle in an environment that forces them to have continued social interaction. In the case of either eventuality, think ahead as to how your student will respond and work on preparing them with tips or direct coaching.

How Are Courses Graded? High school students are often accustomed to regular quizzes, tests, or papers that allow them to demonstrate their knowledge throughout the term. This grading style, although rigorous, provides frequent opportunities for errors and improvement, helping students identify areas where they need to focus more attention. While some college courses may require students to turn work in on a frequent basis across a semester, other courses might only have one or two exams a semester or require a major paper due toward the end. End-of-semester deadlines may seem ideal at the start of the semester, but they can quickly become overwhelming (Merchant and Dintino, 2011). Make sure to stress this point for 2e students who struggle with procrastination and meeting deadlines, as they may be shocked by how strict some of their professors can be regarding late assignments.

Students may also be graded on attendance. The structure of each course may be determined by the building in which it is taken, and it is essential that students are able to navigate campus efficiently (Merchant and Dintino, 2011). Try teaching your students how to use GPS technology on their devices or encouraging them to walk from class to class before the start of the semester. Knowing how to navigate campus in a timely manner is especially important if attendance is monitored, as attendance and participation may be part of their final grade. Students will need to make individualized decisions about attending class and how they will participate.

Time Management

Let's consider how a student's daily schedule may vary from high school to college.

The High School Day—Where Does the Time Go?

How do high school students structure their school day? Many might not reflect on how they spend their time, as the start and end of their day are predetermined. The following chart (see Table 6.2) can help students visualize how they spend their time. It can also be useful for parents, guardians, and transition personnel to understand their students' daily schedules. We have provided example hours for one student, but every student will be different and may spend time on tasks not listed here. Keep in mind that there is no right or wrong way to structure a schedule.

As you can see, the high school day is highly structured, dictating students' locations and activities during various time periods throughout the week. This structure will shift significantly when students transition to college.

Table 6.2 The High School Day

How Much Time Is Spent During School Days	*Example Student Hours*	*Your Hours*
In School?	6	
Getting to and from School?	2	
Playing Sports, Participating in Clubs?	3	
Working, Doing Chores, Volunteering, Caring for Siblings or Relatives?	1	
Studying?	3	
Eating?	1	
Getting Ready for School?	.5	
Getting Ready for Bed?	.5	
Sleeping?	6	
Relaxing (e.g., reading, video games, online)?	1	
Doing Other Things?	0	
TOTAL HOURS	**24**	

The College Day—Where Does the Time Go?

Once students leave high school, they may have less support to develop a well-structured daily schedule. While they might receive more academic work in college, many students also have autonomy and flexibility when scheduling and completing their assignments. For example, a student may take four different courses that meet every Monday, Wednesday, and Friday for an hour each. They might have one class that meets on Tuesday and Thursday for an hour and a half. In some cases, a student might have a laboratory meeting that might take one to three hours per week. There are many different possible schedules, but what do each of these have in common? Lots of open time in a typical student's day! Let us look at a sample student (see Table 6.3) who has four one-hour classes that meet Monday, Wednesday, and Friday.

In college, students need to learn how to use their 'Free Time' block above to complete their homework and take care of daily living tasks, including eating and sleeping. Student-athletes, musicians, and workers may have to balance additional demands as well. In every case, it is extremely important for high school students to begin developing their time management skills early.

The importance of time management skills was emphasized by several 2eASD students interviewed by Reis, Gelbar, and Madaus (2022). When asked about essential skills, time management was consistently mentioned in every interview with participants (Austermann et al., 2023). Several students expressed a wish that they had developed these skills in high school. One student stated, 'The school should have taught me how to manage time better. In high school, we had no free time, so I did not know how to [manage] it better. [High school] and college are two different things' (p. 4435). Another student explained, 'High

Table 6.3 A Possible College Day

How Much Time Is Spent on Monday, Wednesday, and Friday?	Example Student Hours
In Class	4
Free Time	20
TOTAL HOURS	**24**

school was about volume, and college is about reacting to challenges.' To manage his college time demands, this student said, 'I chunk out my time carefully and make sure that if I know I am going to need ten hours to do something, I plan to spend two hours every day on that task and then give it five days' (p. 4435).

Students can benefit from various time management strategies. Numerous time management software programs and apps are available online, but even a simple chart like Table 6.3 can help students structure their day. The chart below shows the schedule of a sample student who is taking four classes (with one lab) and holds a part-time job on campus. This student also has time blocked off for exercise and completing work. While still in high school, you can help your students by working with them to develop charts like these and encouraging them to explore time management systems.

Services for Students with Disabilities: What Are the Differences from High School to College?

Before we discuss the services available for students with disabilities at the college level, let's consider what services students

Table 6.4 A Sample Weekly Schedule

	MON	TUES	WED	THURS	FRI
7–8 AM	Wake up and get ready	Wake up and get ready	Wake up and get ready	Wake up and get ready	Wake up and get ready
8–9 AM	PSYCH		PSYCH		PSYCH
9–10 AM	LIBRARY	MATH	LIBRARY	MATH	LIBRARY
10–11 AM	ENGLISH	MATH	ENGLISH	MATH	ENGLISH
11–12 PM	LIBRARY	LIBRARY	LIBRARY	LIBRARY	LIBRARY
12–1 PM	LUNCH	LUNCH	LUNCH	LUNCH	LUNCH
1–2 PM	HISTORY	JOB	HISTORY	JOB	HISTORY
2–3 PM	JOB	JOB	JOB	JOB	
3–4 PM	WORK OUT	WORK OUT	WORK OUT	WORK OUT	WORK OUT
4–5 PM	WORK OUT	WORK OUT	PSYCH LAB	WORK OUT	WORK OUT
5–6 PM	DINNER	DINNER	DINNER	DINNER	DINNER

Table 6.5 What Types of Services Do You Use Now?

List the services or supports that you receive now (e.g., extended test time, test reader, modified grades, a tutor etc.)	In What Classes Do You Use These?	How Does it Help You?	Who Sets it Up for You?

have in high school. Table 6.5 can help students reflect on the support they receive and how these supports have helped them in high school.

Services at the High School Level

Students with disabilities receive support services under two federal laws, the Individuals with Disabilities Education Act (IDEA) and Section 504 of the Rehabilitation Act of 1973. Below, we examine both and consider what they do for disabled students.

Individuals with Disabilities Education Act

As a teacher, you are likely familiar with IDEA. The IDEA is a federal law that requires states and local school districts to provide special education services to eligible students. Local districts must identify and evaluate referred students for any suspected disabilities. If a student meets eligibility criteria for one or more disability classification, the district is required to provide that student with free and individually appropriate public education at no additional cost to them or their family.

Schools must develop an Individualized Education Program (IEP) for students classified with an educational disability. As described by the name, this document must be individualized to fit each student's particular needs and strengths. The IEP must clearly provide information on the student's present level of performance in a range of academic, behavioral, and functional areas, and list out annual goals for growth. The IEP is required to detail the modifications and accommodations that will be provided to the student, including the location and duration of these services, any assistive technologies that will be supplied, and the identification of the professionals responsible for delivering these services.

While you may be aware of many of the IEP accommodations that students receive in K-12 classrooms, you might not realize that the transition to adulthood is also an essential part of developing an IEP. Starting at age 16, postsecondary goals relating to a student's education, employment, and independent living must be developed and described each year (McGuire, 2010). The student's family or caretakers must be explicitly included as part of the decision-making team. Any IEP-related services end when the student's team (including the family) determines the services are no longer needed, or if the student graduates, drops out, or ages out of public schools.

Section 504 of the Rehabilitation Act of 1973

You may also have experience working with students' 504 plans. Unlike the IDEA, 504s are not considered a part of special education law. Instead, Section 504 is a component of the Vocational Rehabilitation Act of 1973, making it a federal civil rights act designed to prevent discrimination in programs that receive federal financial assistance. There are many students in K-12 schools who need accommodations or modifications to properly access their education but do not need individualized special education services. This is where special education services under Section 504 apply. For example, a student might need extended test time, a quiet room for exams, or assistance with having a quiz read to them. These students are covered under Subpart D of Section 504, and local districts are required to identify students with potential disabilities and to ensure that they receive modifications and accommodations to access their education. Like IEPs, services, accommodations, and/or modifications under a Section 504 plan also can end when the student's team determines the services are no longer needed. However, the provision of 504s is not limited by age and remains applicable across their lifespan as long as individuals are involved in educational or employment settings that receive federal financial assistance. This means that the accommodations specified under 504 plans must also be provided by federal workplaces, colleges, and adult education services offered by local districts.

Services at the College Level

As noted, special education services end when students leave public school. Colleges and universities are not required to provide special education services to disabled students. However, federally funded universities must ensure that qualified disabled students are protected from disability-based discrimination under Subpart E of Section 504 and the Americans with Disabilities Act. While you may assume that this only applies to public universities, many private colleges receive funding in the form of federal grants or federal student aid programs. It is important to note that although Section 504 applies to both K-12 and postsecondary education, the differing requirements of Subpart D and Subpart E change how students can access services and the services that might be offered (Office for Civil Rights, 2011). We will now examine some of these key changes.

Identifying Disabled Students and Determining Eligibility

High schools are required to identify students with potential disabilities and provide comprehensive multidisciplinary evaluations across domains. Colleges and universities do not have similar requirements. Instead, it is up to the individual students to self-identify themselves to the institution. The decision to self-identify is fully up to the student, but without it, the student is not eligible for disability-related services or protection from disability-related discrimination. The student is also responsible for providing documentation that establishes their disability and their disability-related needs. This documentation is paid for at the cost of the individual student, as colleges and universities are not required to provide or pay for evaluations and disability documentation (Evans et al., 2017; McGuire, 2010; Office for Civil Rights, 2011). As many college students already face significant stress, it is no wonder that some might feel as though they are prevented from receiving the support that they need. To ensure that they do not face these challenges, you can encourage students and families to gather all records related to their disability qualification *before the student leaves high school*. This may include test records, reports, documents, and more. Students can then bring this documentation to their university's disability services office to be eligible for continued support.

Qualified Students

In high school, students with disabilities are eligible for Section 504 protections within their local school district. No public school can turn away a student with a 504 based on their disability. In college, under Subpart E, a student with a disability must also be 'otherwise qualified.' In other words, every student, regardless of ability level, must meet the same admissions requirements. They must meet the specified criteria for admission into their chosen majors or degree programs and maintain the same standards as their non-disabled peers to remain enrolled. For example, neurodiverse students need to meet the minimum standard related to grade point average, earned credits, and institutional codes of behavior and student conduct. It is very important to note that while colleges can set these standards, they cannot set them arbitrarily or discriminate against students with disabilities (Evans et al., 2017).

Types of Available Services

If a student is determined to be eligible, they may receive accommodations that enable them to access their education. The regulations of Section 504, Subpart E, state:

> A recipient to which this subpart applies shall make such modifications to its academic requirements as are necessary to ensure that such requirements do not discriminate or have the effect of discriminating, on the basis of handicap, against a qualified handicapped applicant or student. *Academic requirements that the recipient can demonstrate are essential to the instruction being pursued by such student or to any directly related licensing requirement will not be regarded as discriminatory* [emphasis added] within the meaning of this section. Modifications may include changes in the length of time permitted for the completion of degree requirements, substitution of specific courses required for the completion of degree requirements, and adaptation of the manner in which specific courses are conducted.
> (§104.4[a])

In practice, this might mean that a student who struggles to learn a second language or has difficulty with quantitative courses might still be required to complete requirements in these areas if the institution can show that such courses are essential to the plan of study. On the other hand, institutions are encouraged to explore alternative methods and make accommodations that do not compromise the essential program components but provide equitable access. For instance, a student with a disability that significantly impairs their ability to perform in traditional testing formats might be allowed alternative assessments, such as oral exams or extended project work, to demonstrate their proficiency. Additionally, institutions may provide supplemental instructional support, such as tutoring or assistive technology, to help bridge any gaps without altering the core academic requirements.

The Section 504 regulations also note that institutions must provide accommodations related to course examinations, housing, nonacademic services, and auxiliary aids. Regarding auxiliary aids, the regulations state:

> Auxiliary aids may include taped texts, interpreters or other effective methods of making orally delivered materials available to students with hearing impairments, readers in libraries for students with visual impairments, classroom equipment adapted for use by students with manual impairments, and other similar services and actions. Recipients need not provide attendants, individually prescribed devices, readers for personal use or study, or other devices or services of a personal nature.
> (§104.4[d][2])

Note that the regulations clearly state that personal services are not required. Some colleges may offer these services and charge an additional fee because they go beyond the basic requirements of the law.

Familial Involvement

While at the secondary level, the student's family is explicitly part of the decision-making team, they are not included in the decision-making progress related to student services when they enter postsecondary education (Office for Civil Rights, 2011; Thierfeld Brown et al., 2012). Additionally, caregivers do not communicate directly with their children's professors, which may come as a shock to the parents who have assumed responsibility for their children's learning. At the college level, all responsibilities shift to the student, which is why it is so important to prepare students for the transition to college.

Self-Advocacy Skills

Just as it is up to students to decide if they will self-disclose to the institution, it is also up to the student to request specific accommodations. It is within the student's discretion to decide the timing of such requests. Make sure your students know this, as without a request, colleges are not obligated to provide present, future, or retroactive accommodations. Students will not be compensated for the time they lost while learning in ways that were inadequate for them or their needs. Research indicates that early self-disclosure and accommodation lead to better academic outcomes, while delayed requests lead to poorer outcomes (Blasey, Wang, and Blasey, 2023). Additionally, when 2e and other disabled students receive accommodations, they are more likely to earn high grade point averages, stay in college, and graduate (Kim and Lee, 2016; Mamiseishvili and Koch, 2011; Pingry O'Neill, Markward, and French, 2012).

It is crucial to share these positive outcomes with students who are considering attending college to emphasize the importance of self-advocacy. Self-advocacy skills enable students to effectively describe their needs and work with college professors to receive specific accommodations. In the K-12 environment, the school is responsible for providing accommodations, and students do not have to take any action to receive them. At the college level, however, students with disabilities must actively work with their professors to receive accommodations.

When students receives an accommodation letter from the accessibility services office, it is their responsibility to share this letter with their professors. Otherwise, they are not entitled to the requested services. Essentially, the logistics of receiving accommodations, which were handled by adults at the K-12 level, become the student's responsibility in college.

This responsibility and self-advocacy will be important for life beyond college, as the workforce requires a similar process for accommodations. Overall, attending and graduating from college provides an opportunity for students to experience potential financial gain compared to their peers with less education. More importantly, college offers students the chance to pursue areas of interest, gain expertise, and experience self-growth. Let us consider an example of how a set of high school experiences can support a smooth transition to the university environment.

Daniel

Daniel is a senior at a public high school who receives special education services under the classification of ASD. He is academically gifted, with exceptionally high verbal skills, aptitude, and achievement scores. Daniel has specific talents and interests in STEM areas, particularly meteorology. Daniel's elementary school experience was very challenging, as his teachers focused predominantly on his deficits rather than his strengths. However, this began to change when his parents enrolled him in a small, independent school that agreed to focus on his strengths. This shift in mindset dramatically transformed his entire school experience for the better.

By high school, Daniel was back in a small public school that allowed him to take strength-based advanced classes. As his IEP team began to plan his annual meeting, they considered ways to use a strength-based approach to capitalize on his academic talents and prepare him for the transition to postsecondary education. Initially, they struggled to determine which strength-based learning strategies would be the best fit for 2e students like Daniel. The team decided to examine specific practices and experiences that would enable Daniel to excel in high school and prepare for a competitive college environment. In Daniel's case, it was particularly important for his own sense of self-efficacy that his teachers and counselors believed that he had strong academic abilities and talents and could successfully participate in advanced learning opportunities.

At his annual IEP meeting, Daniel shared that only one or two of his prior teachers had recognized his academic talents. However, since transitioning out of elementary school, Daniel received support and confidence from multiple teachers who believed in him. For Daniel, this acknowledgment of his talents was crucial for his personal and academic development and contributed directly to his increased confidence and academic success. To support Daniel's growth, the team recommended that he participate in a summer STEM workshop for talented students, which further reinforced his belief in his abilities and his growing self-awareness of his talents and interests.

Daniel also became involved in various extracurricular activities, including sports, clubs, and academic competitions. He continued to favor STEM activities like robotics, meteorology, and computer clubs and began to develop an interest in arts activities, including band and choir. While he tried multiple clubs, he eventually found the right fit for his talents and interests. His IEP team discussed the significant role that carefully selected extracurricular activities could play in his academic success. They encouraged Daniel to develop a talent plan to document his emerging interests, favorite academic subjects, and rewarding extracurricular activities. This helped him analyze these areas and led to discussions about how his interests might influence his future academic and personal choices.

Daniel's team worked closely with him to determine which academic and enrichment experiences would most likely meet his profile of strengths and interests. Advanced, challenging high school classes in areas of interest were essential for Daniel's development. Since his small high school offered a limited number of advanced courses, the IEP team recommended that Daniel participate in a challenging interest-based independent study program. Additionally, the team discussed the possibility of enrolling in a community college course during his senior year and starting a meteorology club at his school. To support his executive functioning, the team developed specific goals and objectives related to self-regulation and time management.

Ultimately, Daniel and his family decided that attending a four-year college was the right path. He applied to six colleges, including two that offered comprehensive support for autistic individuals, and was accepted to five. Daniel chose to attend a state university with excellent engineering and autism-support programs.

The Importance of Student Self-Determination

Closely related to self-advocacy is the need for self-determination. Thus far, this chapter has emphasized the independence college students have in making choices. As stated previously, students with disabilities have a significant level of autonomy when making decisions about self-disclosure and support services. To be successful, these students need both self-advocacy and self-determination. A definition of self-determination that is commonly considered useful is from Field et al. (1998):

Self-determination is a combination of skills, knowledge, and beliefs that enable a person to engage in goal-directed, self-regulated, autonomous behavior. An understanding of one's strengths and limitations, together with a belief in oneself as capable and effective, are essential to self-determination. When acting on the basis of these skills and attitudes, individuals have greater ability to take control of their lives and assume the role of successful adults.

(p. 115)

In other words, self-determination allows students to develop the autonomy that is necessary to make decisions about their lives. Some key components of this definition relate to students' ability to understand their strengths and weaknesses. In the case of 2e students, this means knowing their talents and challenges. Developing this self-awareness is critical for these students as they navigate their academic and personal lives as adults. Once students have a strong concept of their personal abilities, they can begin to develop and plan goals. Field and Hoffman (2015) created the following graphic that displays how these components work together (6.1).

The importance of self-determination was evident in the interviews of 40 2eASD students conducted by Reis, Gelbar, and Madaus (2022). One student stated that he understood his strengths and his needs so that 'by high school, I understood it a lot better and could control the weaknesses. Rather than let them get out of control, I handled them' (p. 4434). Another student wished that she had learned more in high school about self-advocacy and social skills so that she could interact with professors. She stated: 'You should include things that help students understand resources that are available to them. Overexpose them to services that will help them in the long run' (Austermann et al., 2023, p. 6).

Joe Madaus and colleagues (2022) interviewed 11 professionals involved in providing disability support to 2eASD students. Like the students, this group discussed the

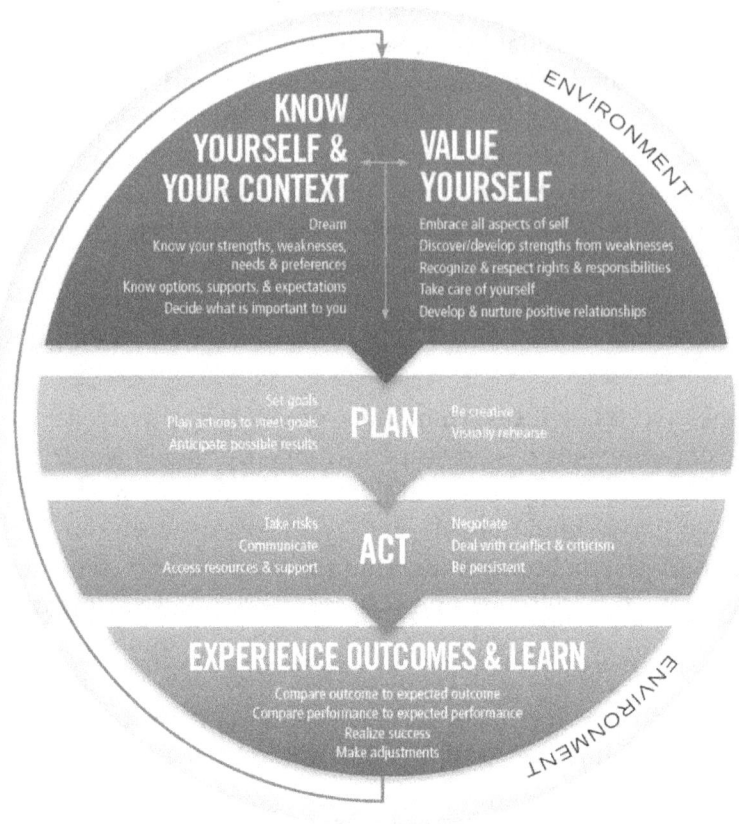

FIGURE 6.1 An Action Model for Self-Determination
(Field and Hoffman, 2015, reprinted with permission)

importance of student self-determination skills. One disability service provider noted that 'these students obviously are very bright . . . so the belief that being bright is enough to be successful and not using the resources is sometimes a stumbling block' (p. 7). Often, 2e students believe that they can overcome their areas of difficulty simply through intelligence. However, to be resilient and well-rounded adults, they will need to strengthen their self-determination. The college environment can support the development of self-determination by giving students the freedom to make decisions and experience the consequences of their actions.

Types of Accommodations Used

Notably, students may not be aware of the accommodations that they can receive if they decide to self-disclose their disabilities to their university. For students like Daniel, finding accommodation and support can mean the difference between graduating with honors or dropping out of college. Newman and colleagues (2011) analyzed data collected from the National Longitudinal Transition Study-2 which tracked a national sample of youth with disabilities from high school into adult life. Sixty percent of the students reported attending postsecondary education, most often at a community, vocational, or technical school (32.3%) or at a four-year college (18.8%). Importantly, only 24% of the students self-disclosed before enrollment, and 4% self-disclosed after enrollment. The vast majority of the remaining students chose to not disclose or did not consider themselves to be disabled. The students who did self-disclose received a range of accommodations and services, as summarized in Table 6.6 (Newman et al., 2011).

Table 6.6 Accommodations and Services Received in College

Type of Accommodation or Service	Percentage Reporting Use in College
Additional time for tests	79.2%
Technology	37%
Tutor	36.8%
Learning/behavior management support	23.3%
Additional time for assignments	23.2%
Different test setting	18.5%
Reader/interpreter/in-class aide	17.4%
Note taker	16.8%
Written materials	10.5%
Physical adaptations to classroom	9.7%
Other testing accommodations	9.4%
Large print/books on tape/braille materials	8.0%
Social work services	8.0%
Case management	7.2%
Independent living supports	6.3%
Early registration	3.2%
Other accommodations or supports	7.5%

Colleges vary in what they can offer students with disabilities. Nevertheless, showing students the list above can help them understand the benefits of self-disclosure. Many supports can be subtly provided if students are worried about others' perceptions. Some supports may be new to students, given their experience in the K-12 classroom. For example, many disabled students do not know that they have access to early registration for classes, which is an accommodation that can be extremely helpful as they plan their courses and schedules.

Shaw, Madaus and, Dukes (2010) summarized some other key points related to accommodations in college:

- Requesting accommodations must be done on a case-by-case and course-by-course basis.
- An accommodation needed for one, or even multiple courses, might not be needed or reasonable in all courses.
- An accommodation approved for one course or at one time in a program of study might not be approved for another course or at another time in a program of study.
- An accommodation might be appropriate for a student in one major but not for a student in another.
- Documentation that was sufficient for determining eligibility for some accommodations might not be sufficient for other accommodation requests.

(p. 53)

If students is unsure about which accommodations would be most beneficial, encourage them to look back at Table 6.5 or complete Table 6.7 below. With the information available about the types of services available in college, students can successfully determine what college-level accommodations are both supportive and realistic.

Table 6.7 What Services Might be Helpful in College?

Type of Service (e.g., extended test time, test reader, quiet test rooms, a tutor etc.)	In What Types of Classes (e.g., math, sciences, history, English, second language)?	How Might it Help You?	How Will it Be Arranged?

Essential Considerations for College-Bound 2e Students

Selecting potential colleges to apply to is a daunting step that involves whittling several thousand postsecondary options down to a list of 5–10 colleges and universities. The diversity of size, location, and cost within colleges and universities is noteworthy. Just as each student is unique, each college possesses its own distinct characteristics. Due to the differences in how accessibility services are provided across campuses, it is important for 2e students and their families to consider different factors as they explore their options. Initially, it may be helpful to detail the types of support and services that the student is receiving in high school. The following questions should be asked:

- ♦ What types of support does this student need?
- ♦ Can these services be provided at this college?
- ♦ Will additional fees be required to access these services?

It is likely that 2e students will require specialized support for social or executive function skills that are not typically afforded to college students. For example, autistic individuals may require the support of a specialized program. Remember, these services often come at an additional expense to the student. Many available resources provide lists of colleges that have specific support programs designed with this group in mind (https://collegeautismspectrum.com/ and https://collegeautismnetwork.org/).

If your student only needs a few accommodations, it may be easier to apply to a wider range of colleges and universities. It is still important to understand the services that an institution can provide and determine whether they will be sufficient to meet the student's needs. To learn more about their options, students and their families can visit many different types of colleges. They should learn about the types of accessibility services offered and ask if they can meet with representatives from disability support offices (see www.cedardatabase.org/ for the contact information for accessibility services at colleges/universities in the U.S.

The 'Apply-To' List

Through their experiences, your students will also gain a clearer understanding of whether they prefer to apply to small, medium, or large schools, as well as their preferred geographic locations and settings. In the process of exploring their options, students should progressively narrow down their list of college choices. Although many colleges are currently test-optional, it's noteworthy that several highly competitive colleges are beginning to reinstate the requirement for standardized test results. Based on the student's grades (and potentially standardized test scores), it's advisable to create a list of colleges that they like and could be accepted to. This list should incorporate 'safety schools' that are highly likely to admit the student and 'reach schools' where acceptance may be more challenging.

Final Steps

After your students has been accepted to one or more schools, they must make their final college decisions. If possible, it may be helpful to visit the schools again and participate in their accepted students' day. This provides the opportunity to meet again with staff at the accessibility/disability office and ask questions about the supports they offer.

If your students have IEP, they will be required to submit a Summary of Performance (SOP) document if they have an IEP. This document is a required part of the IEP process and must consider the input of parents, students, and teachers. It also includes written recommendations from educators and other service providers based on the student's current level of academic achievement. For a 2e student, an SOP should detail specific postsecondary goals that accurately represent the student's potential. This document, along with the student's most recent eligibility evaluations, can be submitted to the accessibility/disability office to determine accommodations they may receive in college.

Conclusion

Let's revisit the quiz that appeared at the beginning of the chapter (Table 6.1). Take it again here.

Reflect on your previous answers (see Appendix H for the answer key). Did any of your choices change? Are there topics you want to explore further? Has this helped you to frame transition discussions with your students and their families?

As you can see, college is a viable and important option for students who have disabilities. It enables them to develop independence and pursue areas of interest in depth. A college degree will also likely lead to higher levels of employment and lifetime earnings. Given the significant differences between high school and college, students with disabilities will face additional challenges in responding to the types and levels of available support services. Careful transition preparation can help support a successful transition and collegiate career for 2e students.

References

Austermann, Q., Gelbar, N. W., Reis, S. M., and Madaus, J. (2023). The transition to college: Lived experiences of academically talented students with autism. *Frontiers in Psychiatry*, 14. https://doi.org/10.3389/fpsyt.2023.1125904

Blasey, J., Wang, C., and Blasey, R. (2023). Accommodation use and academic outcomes for college students with disabilities. *Psychological Reports*, 126(4), 1891–1909. https://doi.org/10.1177/00332941221078011

Broady, K., and Hershbein, B. (2020). Major decisions: What graduates earn over their lifetimes. *The Hamilton Project*. https://orcid.org/0000-0002-2534-8164

Carnevale, A. P., Cheah, B., and Wenzinger, E (2021). *The College Payoff: More Education Doesn't Always Mean More Earnings*. Georgetown University Center on Education and the Workforce. https://cew.georgetown.edu/wp-content/uploads/cew-college_payoff_2021-fr.pdf

Evans, N. J., Broido, E. M., Brown, K. R., and Wilke, A. K. (2017). *Disability in Higher Education: A Social Justice Approach*. Jossey-Bass.

Field, S., and Hoffman, A. (2015). *An Action Model for Self-determination*. www.beselfdetermined.com/model/

Field, S., Martin, J., Miller, R., Ward, M., and Wehmeyer, M. (1998). Self-determination for persons with disabilities: A position statement of the division on career development and transition. *Career Development for Exceptional Individuals*, 21(2), 113–128. https://doi.org/10.1177/088572889802100202

Kim, W. H., and Lee, J. (2016). The effect of accommodation on academic performance of college students with disabilities. *Rehabilitation Counseling Journal*, 60(1), 40–50. https://doi.org/10.177/0034355215605259

Madaus, J., Reis, S., Gelbar, N., Delgado, J., and Cascio, A. (2022). Perceptions of factors that facilitation and impede learning among twice-exceptional college students with autism spectrum disorder. *Neurobiology of Learning and Memory*, 193. https://doi.org/10.1016/j.nlm.2022.107627

Mamiseishvili, K., and Koch, L. C. (2011). First-to-second-year persistence of students with disabilities in postsecondary institutions in the

United States. *Rehabilitation Counseling Bulletin*, 54(2), 93–105. https://doi.org/10.1177/0034355210382580

McGuire, J. M. (2010). Considerations for the transition to college. In S. F. Shaw, J. W. Madaus, and L. L. Dukes, III (Eds.). *Preparing Students with Disabilities for College Success: A Practical Guide to Transition Planning* (pp. 7–36). Brookes Publishing Co.

Merchant, D., and Dintino, M. (2011). Self-advocacy and the transition to college: A curriculum for practitioners. *Keene State College*. https://nextsteps-nh.org/wp-content/uploads/Self-advocacy-and-the-Transition-to-College-12-13-2011.pdf

Newman, L., Wagner, M., Knokey, A. M., Marder, C., Nagle, K., Shaver, D., and Wei, X. (2011). *The Post-high School Outcomes of Young Adults with Disabilities up to 8 Years After High School: A Report from the National Longitudinal Transition Study-2 (NLTS2)*. National Center for Special Education Research. www.nlts2.org/reports/2011_09_02/nlts2_report_2011_09_02_complete.pdf

Office for Civil Rights. (2011). *Students with Disabilities Preparing for Postsecondary Education: Know Your Rights and Responsibilities*. U.S. Department of Education. www2.ed.gov/about/offices/list/ocr/transition.html

Pingry O'Neill, L. N., Markward, M. J., and French, J. P. (2012). Predictors of graduation among college students with disabilities. *Journal of Postsecondary Education and Disability*, 25(1), 21–36. https://files.eric.ed.gov/fulltext/EJ970017.pdf

Reis, S., Gelbar, N., and Madaus, J. (2022). Pathways to academic success: Specific strength-based teaching and support strategies for twice exceptional high school students with autism spectrum disorder. *Gifted Education International*, 39(3), 378–400. https://doi.org/10.1177/02614294221124197

Section 504 of the Rehabilitation Act of 1973, 29 U.S.C. sec 794 www2.ed.gov/policy/rights/reg/ocr/edlite-34cfr104.html#S44

Shattuck, P. T., Narendorf, S. C., Cooper, B., Sterzing, P. R., Wagner, M., and Taylor, J. L. (2012). Postsecondary education and employment among youth with an autism spectrum disorder. *Pediatrics*, 129(6), 1042–1049. https://doi.org/10.1542/peds.2011-2864

Shaw, S. F., Madaus, J. W., and Dukes, L. L. (Eds.). (2010). *Preparing Students with Disabilities for College Success: A Practical Guide to Transition Planning*. Paul H. Brookes Publishing Company.

Thierfeld Brown, J., Wolf, L. E., King, L., and Kukiela Bork, G. R. (2012). *The Parent's Guide to College for Students on the Autism Spectrum*. AAPC Publishing.

U.S. Bureau of Labor Statistics (2024, February). *Employment Status of the Civilian Noninstitutional Population by Disability Status and Selected Characteristics, 2023 Annual Averages.* www.bls.gov/news.release/disabl.t01.htm

7
Concluding Thoughts

Introduction

We hope we have convinced you to use strength-based pedagogy in your classroom. More importantly, we want to emphasize the value of recognizing and leveraging the unique talents of your 2e students. By focusing on students' strengths and talents rather than their deficits, we can create a more positive and enjoyable learning experience for all. While strength-based learning benefits all students, it is especially advantageous for neurodiverse students. Discovering and building on their interests enhances their confidence, self-esteem, and motivation by highlighting what they do well.

To effectively use strength-based pedagogy, start by creating an inviting classroom environment where students can explore their interests and passions. Offer various entry points, resources, and choices to allow students to engage in projects that integrate their interests and abilities. This book provides numerous examples of how you can leverage a student's strengths to help them master challenging and daunting content. By offering dually differentiated content, you provide multiple pathways for students to apply their strengths and abilities to complex lessons and assignments. We suggest combining enrichment and talent development opportunities to motivate students to understand

DOI: 10.4324/9781003511861-7

how specific skills can help them pursue high-interest areas. In essence, helping students understand why they should learn a skill is the key to supporting their academic futures.

We also discussed incorporating a strength-based goal to develop the strengths of students in special education programs. This may involve the process of collaborative goal setting between educators, students, and parents to create tailored learning plans. The first step to this is, again, taking the time to understand and develop your students' interests, which leads to more engaged learning. In earlier chapters, we reviewed the use of various strategies, including interest inventories, observations, and interviews, to help your students identify their strengths and interests. It amazes us how rarely students are asked what and how they'd like to learn. When asked, they're often so surprised that they don't know how to respond. Once interests are identified, it is essential to student's time for further study through specialized instruction, projects, and activities. As we mentioned, project-based learning, both independently and in small groups, enhances motivation, time management, and executive functioning skills, all necessary for future academic success.

We have also highlighted the importance of various types of enrichment and extracurricular activities in further developing students' interests, social understanding, and direction for future programs. Our research with highly successful students with ASD showed that over 90% participated in extracurricular activities (Reis, Gelbar, and Madaus, 2021). These activities, including sports, clubs, and competitions, significantly impacted their strongest areas of interest.

While many students preferred individual activities, others enjoyed the relationships developed through teamwork. It often took time for neurodiverse students to find activities that matched their interests and needs, trying several before finding the right fit.

Using Strength-based Learning to Promote Socioemotional Well-being and Success

Students who are 2e face various challenges and threats to their social and emotional well-being, which can hinder the development of their unique talents. These differences can make it difficult for teachers to understand their unique profiles and needs. We urge you to consider that these students are individuals and what works for one twice-exceptional student may not work for another. Students who are 2e may experience asynchronous development, meaning that some, but not all, of these students will have heightened sensitivity and complex internal experiences. Some of these students are easily overwhelmed and may be prone to outbursts that result from overstimulation or anxiety. It is critical that teachers of 2e students work to create a safe academic environment that can support students' productivity, creativity, and sense of well-being. Providing academic support while also addressing their social and emotional needs is essential.

Rather than focusing on the negative characteristics commonly associated with 2e students, we encourage you to focus on their positive attributes. This positive approach can provide a welcome change for students who may be seeking a more open and supportive teaching style. Twice-exceptional students often experience underachievement, leading educators to overlook their abilities while failing to identify them for gifted program services. By recognizing their talents, you can implement tools and strategies that enhance their overall academic success.

We hope that you are able to maintain open lines of communication with the parents of your students who are 2e. Parents can provide valuable insights into their children's unique gifts and talents, helping you connect classroom activities with the events that influence their behavior. This understanding can empower you to respond effectively to your student's needs, reducing negative and disruptive behaviors. Additionally, be aware of the issues that may stem from a lack of intellectual stimulation. Your students who are 2e may feel under-challenged in school, which could escalate their emotional and behavioral problems. Whenever possible, please consider offering advanced content, talent development, and enrichment opportunities to your students. These types of activities will help them build the necessary skills to excel in advanced work through improved executive function and self-regulation. Encouraging interest-based enrichment activities can enhance students' self-esteem and reduce frustration. Demonstrating to your students that you recognize that they are smart and have unique strengths that contribute to your classroom is critically important.

Throughout this book, we have emphasized the need to create appropriate, safe, and engaging environments. To summarize:

- The **academic/intellectual environment** should provide options for interest and strength-based learning.
- The **social environment** should offer opportunities for students to spend time with peers who accept them and share their interests.
- The **emotional environment** should enable students to feel psychologically safe and supported.
- The **creative environment** should give students a place where ideas, creative products, and brainstorming can emerge.

Identifying Students Strengths and Interests

To start with strength-based strategies that contribute to academic success, begin with interest identification and development strategies. Integrating self-reflective practices into learning can help students think about their interests, strengths, and goals. This self-reflection provides valuable insights into their personal inclinations and academic aspirations, helping them align their education with their talents and passions. Engaging in conversations about your students likes and interests will encourage them to share important information about their academic and personal goals. Identifying their learning passions can help you to identify key strengths and opportunities to advance their gifts.

We talked about the use of several easy-to-administer interest assessments that you can use with your students. Allowing students to reflect on their goals through surveys and assessments will provide you with a broad picture of how to help develop their talents. You may consider taking an adult interest survey to assess your personal passions and goals, helping you understand the process from a student perspective. Assessing your student's interests demonstrates that you value their individuality, which can motivate them to engage in their education.

Keeping a log of which enrichment activities your students liked can be helpful for planning talent enrichment for 2e students. Exposing students to a variety of topics, ideas, and projects they can pursue in their area of interest is critical. As you get started, have your students begin with projects that are smaller projects to avoid overwhelming them as they begin their explorations. Encouraging students to create their own talent portfolios, whether physical or electronic, allows them to compile and store details about their strengths and passions. These portfolios should categorize information into abilities, interests, and learning styles, and be reviewed regularly. This reflection enables students to identify and pursue talent development opportunities and enrichment experiences, either independently or with support. Over time, teachers will develop a diverse collection of ideas, materials, and activities that cater to students' favorite enrichment activities. This resource will be beneficial for future students and can be shared with other teachers interested in implementing the SEM.

Planning Enrichment Experiences that Work for All Students

Using parts or all of the SEM will enable you to help students develop their interests and strengths and engage in enrichment learning beyond the regular curriculum. Many teachers have used the Enrichment Triad Model to structure lessons and organize different types of strength-based learning. The Triad includes three types of enrichment:

1. **Type I Enrichment:** Exposes students to topics that can excite and engage them in a variety of areas.
2. **Type II Enrichment:** Provides training to promote thinking and feeling processes through novel materials and methods.

3. **Type III Enrichment:** Enables students to develop skills in an area of interest while creating an authentic and creative product.

We believe that the use of the SEM is especially important for your neurodiverse learners who demonstrate heightened academic abilities. It is possible that these 2e students have not been exposed to academic opportunities that enable them to explore and develop their interests as desired. As you work with them, these students will recognize that your method of developing their interests is different from the deficit-based perspectives that they have previously encountered. SEM activities can help them overcome negative self-concepts that have stemmed from years of having their needs and interests overlooked. The SEM offers students from a variety of cultural, linguistic, and economic backgrounds the opportunity to pursue meaningful topics of interest. By using the SEM and Enrichment Triad Model, you are practicing inclusive educational practices that will promote the academic success of all students in your classroom.

You can also integrate various types of thinking skills and problem-solving activities, as well as a few 'how to' methods, as part of your strength-based learning options. For example, you might teach younger students to brainstorm ideas for a short pop-up book based on their interests and then create it. This incorporates strength-based strategies that fall under Type I and II enrichment. Type II activities also include other advanced instruction in students' self-selected areas of interest, preparing them for specific Type III Enrichment activity.

Project-Based Learning and Type III Enrichment-Using These in Your Classroom

As we have stated, an important strength-based strategy to use with your students is project-based learning. This approach allows students to investigate self-selected problems using methods employed by professionals in their areas of interest. When teachers guide students in engaging with advanced-level content, it can enhance their desire to grow across academic content areas. Showing students how these activities may be implemented in their community can lead to a positive impact beyond the confines of your classroom. When your students are invited to engage in producing creative research, they will be more successful in their academic and personal futures (Reis and Peters, 2021). These opportunities will prepare your students for success in high school and in college. Based on decades of research, we can assure you there is no need to withhold any opportunities that involve developing your students' areas of strength. Keep emphasizing the talents of your students who are 2e, as this will improve their educational outcomes and attitudes toward school. We hope you will engage in frequent discussions with your students about their areas of interest. Remember that asking open-ended questions can encourage students to reflect more on their talents. When possible, allow your students to share stories and invite them to discuss their beliefs about how you can help them flourish.

Using strength-based strategies does not mean that you need to be an expert in all of your student's areas of interest. Instead, your role is to help students learn how to learn, focus on a topic or problem, and develop the skills needed to solve those problems. Assisting students in identifying resources to improve their problem-solving and executive function skills will equip them with invaluable lifelong abilities.

You can also demonstrate how to start the process of mindful assessment of one's own work. For example, your students may need help developing critical thinking skills that allow them to evaluate the outcomes of their work, process, and product. Remember, students who are engaged in creative productive work almost always view their studies as interesting, beneficial, and relevant to their emerging understanding of their own identities. Joseph Renzulli (1977) discusses the ways that task commitment and identity emerge over time in his work on the Three Ring Conception of Giftedness and the Enrichment Triad Model. Over time, these projects have enhanced student motivation and provided them with opportunities to learn how to work as professionals in their fields of interest.

Transitioning to College

The transition to college will be difficult for 2e students and it is likely that they will need a supportive teacher to help prepare them for postsecondary education. As we have discussed, several differences exist between college and high school expectations. Some key questions students should consider when transitioning to college include the type of college they should attend, the majors offered, the location, and the availability of disability services. Walking students through a discussion of these topics can help them with future decision-making. Developing time management skills is crucial as students prepare for college. Encourage your students to consider how they allocate time to daily activities. This approach will teach them to break down assignments, create schedules, and manage their workload over time.

We cannot stress often enough that students who are 2e receive different support for their disabilities in their K–12 education compared to college. Students should examine the support they receive during their K–12 years and consider what will be available for them in college. Once enrolled in higher education, they will need to request the accommodations that they require. Although colleges are not required to provide special education services, they are prevented from discriminating against students with disabilities. When students advocate for themselves, they are more likely to access the support that they need and achieve academic success.

Teaching students to develop self-determination skills can help them become more autonomous in college. Students need to be aware of their own profiles, including their abilities, weaknesses, goals, and behavior patterns. This awareness will enable them to make necessary adjustments to achieve their self-selected goals.

Wasted Talents

Far too many talents are wasted, ignored, and undeveloped in our society. If adults ultimately choose not to develop their talents, there is little that we can do as educators to reverse that trend. But while students are in school, we can and should do everything we can to identify, preserve, and develop students' talents and potential. Too few students with disabilities have opportunities to participate in strength-based learning opportunities. Joe Renzulli and other educators who advocate for enrichment education have spent decades promoting these projects, resources, and academic challenges. By providing these opportunities, we can help all students, especially those with disabilities, reach their full potential.

We have all worked for decades to reverse the trend of underachievement, and yet, we still hear daily from parents of high potential and gifted 2e students about the obstacles their children face in school. We ask for your help to reverse this trend. Recently, a call from a dean at a competitive university brought this issue to the forefront once again. The dean explained that his son, a gifted student with ASD, had recently dropped out of his second year of engineering—a lifelong dream for him—due to social challenges he faced in college. This brilliant student had been accepted into a highly competitive engineering program. Despite his efforts to obtain help and request simple accommodations, such as a single room and reduced course loads, he was unable to find the support he needed to succeed. He eventually quit college, adamant that he would not return. We learned later that his mental and physical health were suffering. We grieve the loss of his potential contributions to society, and this scenario repeats itself again and again.

Conclusion

In this chapter, we have discussed ways to engage and motivate students by focusing on their interests and helping them develop thinking and planning skills to pursue those interests. Research on the Enrichment Triad and SEM Model suggests that talent development opportunities effectively motivate students to pursue high-interest areas and actively engage in their learning (Reis and Peters, 2021). In short, high levels of engagement and joyful learning emerge when students take time to develop and pursue their interests. We will explore this message in greater depth in the next chapter.

In closing, we ask you to become the change agents who support the hopes and dreams of these young people. You are the most important academic mentor in their lives for the time they are in your classroom, and you can be the teacher that they remember, the one that helps to create their future by recognizing and developing their strengths and interests so they can use their talents to contribute to our society and find personal satisfaction and happiness.

References

Reis, S. M., Gelbar, N. W., and Madaus, J. W. (2021). Understanding the academic success of academically talented college students with autism spectrum disorders. *Journal of Autism and Developmental Disorders.* https://doi.org/10.1007/s10803-021-05290-4

Reis, S. M., and Peters, P. M. (2021). Research on the schoolwide enrichment model: Four decades of insights, innovation, and evolution. *Gifted Education International*, 37(2), 109–141. https://doi.org/10.1177/0261429420963987

Renzulli, J. S. (1977). The Enrichment Triad Model: A plan for developing defensible programs for the gifted and talented. *Gifted Child Quarterly*, 21(2), 227–233. https://doi.org/10.1177/001698627702100216

Appendices

Appendix A
Developing Your Own Plan

It is now time to consider developing your own plan for how you will be able to increase your self-regulation. It may require a combination of various strategies that have been introduced as a part of this module. Before you begin thinking about your own plan, you may want to consider the following two questions.

1. What are some common self-regulation strategies that have worked well for other successful students and can help you to be successful in school if you stick with them?
2. What are some individual skills that you must develop personally to be successful in school and life?

Look at the list below . . . which Self-Regulation strategies do you think will work for you?

Personal

Organizing and transforming information
- ☐ Outlining
- ☐ Summarizing
- ☐ Rearrangement of materials
- ☐ Highlighting
- ☐ Flashcards/index cards
- ☐ Raw pictures, diagrams, chart
- ☐ Webs/mapping

Goal setting and planning/standard setting
- ☐ Sequencing, timing, completing
- ☐ Time management and pacing

Keeping records and monitoring
- ☐ Note-taking
- ☐ Lists of errors made
- ☐ Record of marks
- ☐ Portfolio, keeping all drafts of assignments

Rehearsing and memorizing (written or verbal; overt or covert)
- ☐ Mnemonic devices
- ☐ Teaching someone else the material
- ☐ Making sample questions
- ☐ Using mental imagery
- ☐ Using repetition

Behavioral

Self-evaluating (checking quality or progress)
- ☐ Task analysis (What does the teacher want me to do? What do I want out of it?)
- ☐ Self-instructions; enactive feedback
- ☐ Attentiveness

Self-consequating
- ☐ Treats to motivate; self-reinforcement.
- ☐ Arrangement or imagination of punishments; delay of gratification

Environmental

Environmental structuring
- ☐ Selecting or arranging the physical setting
- ☐ Isolating/ eliminating or minimizing distractions
- ☐ Break up study periods and spread them over time

Seeking social assistance
- ☐ Ask a friend, a teacher, or another adult.
- ☐ Follow the lead of a student who is successful.

Seeking information from nonsocial sources
- ☐ Go to the library, read a book or a magazine article.
- ☐ Watch a TV show or find it on the web.
- ☐ Find examples out in the real world.

Reviewing records
- ☐ Reread notes, tests, and textbooks

Appendix B
Total Talent Portfolio

Appendices ◆ 179

Total Talent Portfolio
for

_____

| Month | Year |

My Portfolio of Interests, Talents and Achievements

This Total Talent Portfolio belongs to:	
My Teachers' Names:	
Kindergarten:	1st Grade:
2nd Grade:	3rd Grade
4th Grade:	

TOTAL TALENT PORTFOLIO For:

Status Information

	K		1		2		3		4	
	I Like This	I am Good at This	I Like This	I am Good at This	I Like This	I am Good at This	I Like This	I am Good at This	I Like This	I am Good at This
Subject Areas:										
Reading										
Writing										
Spelling										
Mathematics										
Social Studies										
Science										
Art										
Music										
Physical Education										
Other:										
Class Activities I Like:										
Talking with Projects Others										
Listening to the Teacher										
Answering Questions										
Simulations										
Games										
Doing Worksheets										
Doing Projects										
Computers										
Working in a Group										
Pretending										
Working Alone										
Peer Tutoring										
Learning Centers										
Mentorship										
Other:										
Assignments I Like:										
Writing										
Talking										
Hands-on Activities										
Art projects										
Displays										
Drama/Performing										
Helping Others										
Multi-media: video, audio, computer, overhead										
Other:										

TOTAL TALENT PORTFOLIO For:

My Interests and Talents

Interests:	K	1	2	3	4
Performing Arts					
Creative Writing & Journalism					
Mathematics					
Business/Management					
Athletics					
History					
Social Action					
Fine Arts & Crafts					
Science					
Technology					
Other:					
Specific Interests:					

Talents	K	1	2	3	4
This year my talents/interests were:					
Next year I would like to investigate:					

TOTAL TALENT PORTFOLIO For:

TALENT DEVELOPMENT ACTION RECORD

DIRECTIONS: <u>Clusters</u>: Record the date and title of the cluster the student participated in. If the title is not descriptive of the cluster subject, include a brief description as well.

<u>Compacting</u>: Be sure to include the date and curriculum area compacted, as well as the replacement activities substituted.

	ENRICHMENT CLUSTERS	CURRICULUM COMPACTING
K		
1	ENRICHMENT CLUSTERS	CURRICULUM COMPACTING
2	ENRICHMENT CLUSTERS	CURRICULUM COMPACTING
3	ENRICHMENT CLUSTERS	CURRICULUM COMPACTING
4	ENRICHMENT CLUSTERS	CURRICULUM COMPACTING

TOTAL TALENT PORTFOLIO For:

Action Information

	Activities & Lessons I Do Outside of School	Type IIIs & Projects I Did at Home
K		
1		
2		
3		
4		

Appendix C
If I Ran the School

If I Ran the School
AN INTEREST INVENTORY

Developed by Deborah E. Burns   Designed by Del Siegle

Name: _____

Grade: _____ Teacher: _____

If I ran the school, I would choose to learn about these 10 things. I have thought about my answers very carefully and I have circled my best ideas for right now.

I AM REALLY INTERESTED IN:

SCIENCE

The Stars and Planets	The Weather
Birds	Electricity, Light, and Energy
Dinosaurs and Fossils	Volcanoes and Earthquakes
Life in the Ocean	Insects
Trees, Plants, and Flowers	Reptiles
The Human Body	Rocks and Minerals
Monsters and Mysteries	Machines and Engines
Animals and Their Homes	Diseases and Medicine
Outer Space, Astronauts, and Rockets	Chemistry and Experiments

SOCIAL STUDIES

Families	Problems We Have in Our Town
The Future	Holidays
Our Presidents	Native Americans, Asian Americans, Hispanics, and African Americans
The United States	
Other Countries	Explorers
History and Long Ago Times	People Who Live and Work in Our Town
Famous Men and Women	Travel and Transportation

Figure 22. *If I Ran the School Interest* survey.

MATH

- Math Games and Puzzlers
- Measuring Lines, Liquids, Weight
- Shapes and Sizes
- Buying and Money
- Calculators and Computers
- Building
- Counting and Numbering
- Calendars and Time
- Math Stories and Problems

LANGUAGE ARTS

- Writing a Book
- Writing Poems
- Writing Plays and Skits
- Writing Newspapers
- Making Speeches
- Sign Language
- Making a Book
- Comic and Cartoon Strips
- Letter Writing
- Spanish and French
- Talking and Listening to Stories
- Making a New Game or Puzzle

ARTS

- Cartoons
- Art Projects
- Painting
- Clay
- Acting
- Dancing
- Drawing
- Writing Music
- Photography
- Movies
- Puppets
- Radio and Television
- Famous Artists and Their Work
- Making New Toys
- Magic
- Mime

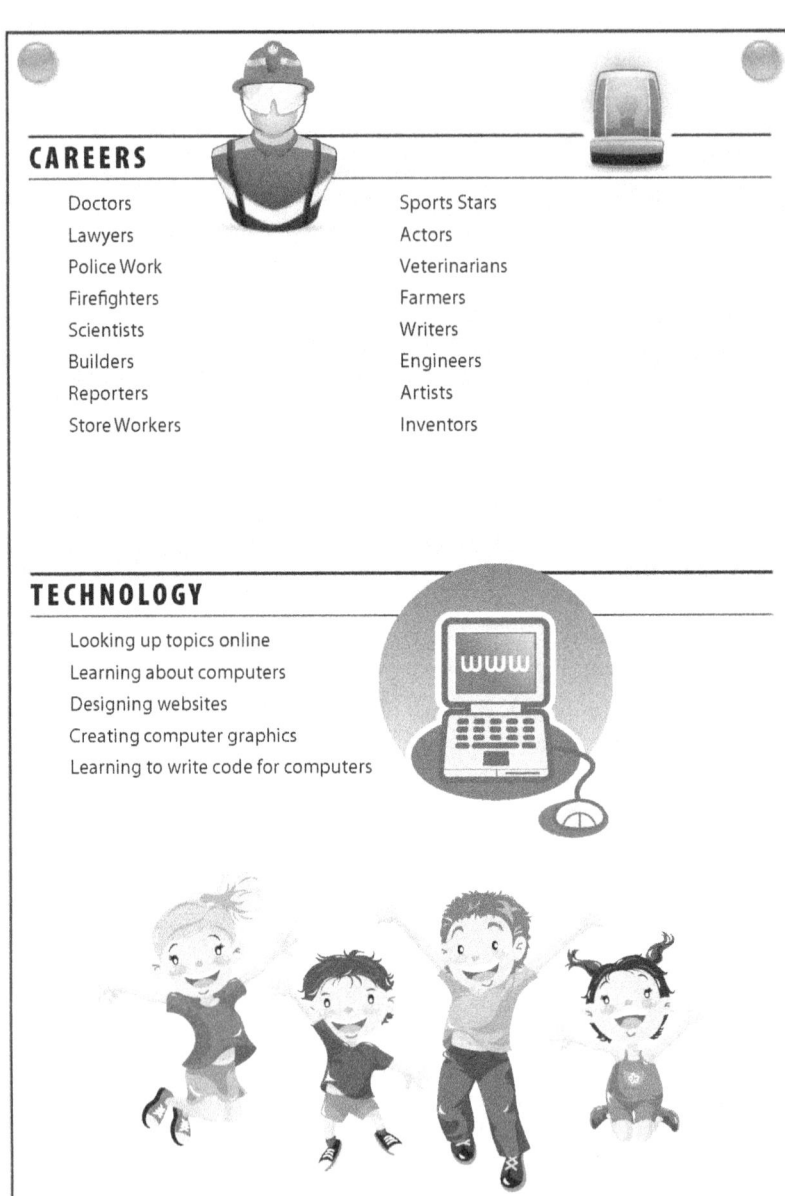

CAREERS

- Doctors
- Lawyers
- Police Work
- Firefighters
- Scientists
- Builders
- Reporters
- Store Workers
- Sports Stars
- Actors
- Veterinarians
- Farmers
- Writers
- Engineers
- Artists
- Inventors

TECHNOLOGY

- Looking up topics online
- Learning about computers
- Designing websites
- Creating computer graphics
- Learning to write code for computers

Appendix D
Interest-A-Lyzer

Interests, Connections, Purpose

Megan Gless
Dr. Joseph S. Renzulli
Dr. Michele Femc-Bagwell

Name: _____
Grade: _____
Age: _____

Dear Student,

The purpose of this survey is for you and your teacher to become familiar with your interests, which will lead to connections with others. No answer is the wrong answer, which is what makes this survey so great! It is also completely confidential, only your teacher will see it. However, you may wish to discuss with others afterwards, that is up to you!

Take your time to answer each question honestly, really think about what you enjoy and wish to focus on this year. The hope is that throughout the year, you will be able to engage in projects either individual or with others that involve your interests and strengths.

You should think about things that interest you now, but also what you would like to try if you had the opportunity to do so.

This survey is all about YOU! Please don't think about what others might be writing. Let this come from your heart, your interests and what you want to do.

If I were to make a YouTube video, it would be about . . . 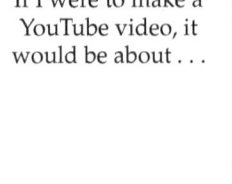	A problem I wish I could solve is . . .	I've only tried it once or twice but I really enjoy . . .
I am the "go to" person when my friends need help with . . .	If I could meet any three people (past or present, famous or not) I would like to meet . . . 1. 2. 3. 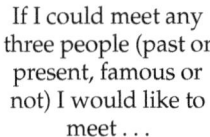	If I could plan my own unit in school, it would be about . . .

Interests, Connections, Purpose

After school you can find me doing or you can find me at . . .	I made my own invention! It is . . . It does . . .	Most people don't know this about me, but I really enjoy . . .
If I were to write a book it would be about . . . Genre: Title: About:	If I won first place in a talent show it would be for . . .	If I could have my own business, it would be . . . (What is being sold? Is it a store? Service?)

Appendices ◆ 193

Activity		I ENJOY doing this and want to do it more …	I have tried this before and want to try it again …	I have NOT tried this, but I am interested in trying it!	I have tried this before but it wasn't my favorite …	I am NOT interested in trying this …
Painting or drawing						
Planting a garden						
Helping animals						
Building with Legos						
Learning robotics						
Learning to code						
Playing sports						
Play an instrument or sing						

Photography								
Creating comics								
Going to a play or musical								
Figuring out puzzles (jigsaw etc.)								
Cooking or baking								
Doing science experiments								
Creating jewelry or clothes								
Helping the environment								
Playing math games								

(Continued)

(Continued)

Activity	I ENJOY doing this and want to do it more ...	I have tried this before and want to try it again ...	I have NOT tried this, but I am interested in trying it!	I have tried this before but it wasn't my favorite ...	I am NOT interested in trying this ...
Read or watch the news					
Learning another language					
Learning about cultures or places					
Creating a fitness routine					

Secondary Interest-A-Lyzer

Basic Biographic Questions

 1. Currently, what are your three favorite subjects?

 2. Currently, what are your favorite topics to study?

 3. Do you currently belong to any clubs/organizations in school? (explain/describe)

 4. Do you currently belong to any clubs/organizations out of school? (explain/describe)

 5. Do you currently play any sports or belong to a sports team? (explain/describe)

 6. What are your favorite traditions, holidays, or celebrations?

 7. Do you belong to any political action/involvement groups?

Top 3–5

1. The Science Department is hosting a science summit with guest speakers who are experts in their fields of study. What are the top 3–5 presentations you would like to attend? Rank your choices 1, 2, or 3 in order of preference.

   ___ Health and Medicine
   ___ Vaccinations and Epidemics
   ___ Nutrition and Exercise
   ___ Reproduction and Sexuality
   ___ Space Exploration/Astronomy
   ___ Mechanical Engineering—Automobiles
   ___ Mechanical Engineering—Weaponry
   ___ The Science of Cosmetics
   ___ Solar, Mechanical, Wind, and Fossil Fuel Energies
   ___ Genetic Engineering
   ___ Endangered Species
   ___ Forensic Science/Medicine
   ___ Robotics and Artificial Intelligence
   ___ Farming and Agriculture
   ___ Genetically Modified Foods
   ___ Weather Patterns and Natural Disasters
   ___ Environmental Issues—Pollution
   ___ Environmental Issues—Global Warming and Climate Change

2. You have an opportunity to contribute to an online newspaper. Every day, people from all over the world will submit articles to be posted for followers and subscribers. What column would you like to be written? Rank your choices 1, 2, or 3 in order of preference.

___ Cooking and Baking
___ Restaurant Reviews
___ Nutrition
___ Travel
___ Fashion
___ Local Politics
___ National Politics
___ International Politics
___ Science and Medicine
___ Celebrity Gossip Columns
___ Book Reviews
___ Crosswords, Sudoku, Math Puzzles
___ Interior Design/Décor
___ TV/Movie Reviews
___ Music/Concert Review
___ Cartoons/Jokes
___ Technology
___ Cars/Motorcycles/Automobiles

3. You have been asked to participate in the production of a major film. You can decide both what the film is about and your role in the production of the film.

   a. What type of film would this be? List your top three choices for the type of film.

   ☐ Documentary
   ☐ Musical
   ☐ Biography
   ☐ Mystery/Detective
   ☐ Horror
   ☐ Animated (Pixar, Cartoon, CG)
   ☐ Superhero
   ☐ Crime/Gang Drama
   ☐ Science Fiction/Fantasy
   ☐ Comedy
   ☐ Romantic Comedy
   ☐ Drama
   ☐ Intended for Teenagers
   ☐ War-Related (Anti-War) Drama
   ☐ Action-Packed
   ☐ Zombie

b. What role do you want in completing the film?

☐ Director
☐ Screen Writer
☐ Script/Set Supervisor
☐ Food and Beverage Supplier
☐ Costume/Make Up Artist
☐ Set Design
☐ Set Construction
☐ Lighting Specialist
☐ Casting Director

☐ Camera Operator
☐ Sound Effects
☐ Special Effects (CG)
☐ Stage Manger
☐ Stage Crew
☐ Lead Actor
☐ Extra
☐ Stunt Person
☐ Location Scout

> 4. Being a teenager is tricky as you face a lot of issues that you don't always have time to explore or discuss.

   a. What social issues would you like to be able to learn more about? Select your top 3–5 options, ranking your choices 1, 2, or 3 in order of preference.

   ___ Human Trafficking
   ___ Immigration/Asylum Seekers, Refugees
   ___ Public Health Care
   ___ Tuition-Free College/University
   ___ Plastic Consumption and Waste
   ___ Gun Violence (Domestic, School Shootings)
   ___ Terrorism
   ___ Legalized Marijuana
   ___ LGBTQ Rights, Issues, and Identity
   ___ Rights, Issues, and Identity about Disabilities
   ___ Mental Health Rights, Issues, and Identity
   ___ Race, Racism, Stereotypes, and Ethnocentrism
   ___ Poverty, Wage Gaps, and Income Inequality
   ___ Environmental Sustainability

___ Voter Restriction
___ HIV/AIDS
___ Access to Clean Drinking Water
___ Prison Industrial Complex Mass Incarceration
___ Vegetarianism/Veganism
___ Access to Health Care/Clinics
___ Abortion/Reproductive Rights Bullying (Cyber Bullying In-School Bullying)

b. What issues, if any, would you like to pursue in community-action groups?

☐ Human Trafficking
☐ Immigration/Asylum Seekers, Refugees
☐ Public Health Care
☐ Tuition-Free College/University
☐ Gun Violence (Domestic, School Shootings)
☐ Terrorism
☐ Legalized Marijuana
☐ Voter Restriction
☐ HIV/AIDS
☐ Access to Clean Drinking Water
☐ Prison Industrial Complex Mass Incarceration
☐ Abortion/Reproductive Rights
☐ Bullying (Cyber Bullying In-School Bullying)
☐ LGBTQ Rights, Issues, and Identity
☐ Handicapped Rights, Issues, and Identity
☐ Plastic Consumption and Waste
☐ Mental Health Rights, Issues, and Identity
☐ Race, Racism, Stereotypes, and Ethnocentrism
☐ Poverty, Wage Gaps, and Income Inequality
☐ Environmental Sustainability
☐ Vegetarianism/Veganism
☐ Access to Health Care/Clinics

Open Ended (List)

1. You've been asked to organize an afterschool event for other high school students. You have an unlimited budget and very few requirements. However, you have to arrange three guest appearances. Who are your top three presenters/speakers/performers? What do they do/what are they known for?
   a.
   b.
   c.

2. You are only allowed to take five pictures on your next trip/vacation. What are they of? Why?
   a.
   b.
   c.
   d.
   e.

3. Our school is putting together a time capsule to be opened in 200 years. The time capsule will teach future generations what it was like to be alive right now. What three personal possessions do you include in your time capsule that represent who you are?
   a.
   b.
   c.

4. A mentorship program is being arranged at your school to allow you to work with a person in the community that is a professional in an occupation/job you may be interested in. What are three occupations that you would like to explore with a mentor?
   a.
   b.
   c.

5. What are your three favorite books? Briefly explain what these books are about.
   a.
   b.
   c.

6. What social media websites do you use?
   a.
   b.
   c.

7. What are the top three blogs/websites (that are not social media related) do you spend the most free time using?
   a.
   b.
   c.

8. What are your three TV favorite shows/series?
   a.
   b.
   c.

9. What are your three favorite movies?
   a.
   b.
   c.

10. What are your three favorite weekend activities (even if you do not do these regularly)? Or, on your weekends what do you wish you had more time to do?
    a.
    b.
    c.

Open Ended (Explain)

 1. You are tired of all the course offerings at your school. Your principal has asked for student input to identify new course selections/offerings.

   a. You can develop and design the perfect course for people who have similar interests as you. What would the course be called? What is taught in this class?

   b. You can modify a class that already exists. What class would you change? What do you change about it?

 2. You're a photographer creating a "themed" Instagram page. What is the theme of the account?

 3. If you could have dinner with any two people you admire—past or present, alive or dead—who would it be? Why did you choose these people? What one question would you ask?

Person A.

Question:

Appendices ◆ 205

Person B.

Question:

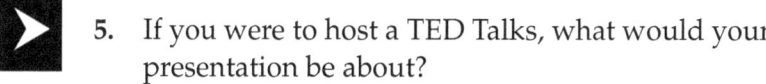
4. If given the opportunity to FaceTime/Skype/Video Chat with anybody alive today for one hour, who would you connect with? Why?

5. If you were to host a TED Talks, what would your presentation be about?

> 6. If you were to create/edit one Wikipedia entry, what would it be about?

7. Imagine it is possible to learn a foreign language instantly. What top two languages would you like to instantly be able to speak? Why?

Appendix E
Primary Interest-A-Lyzer

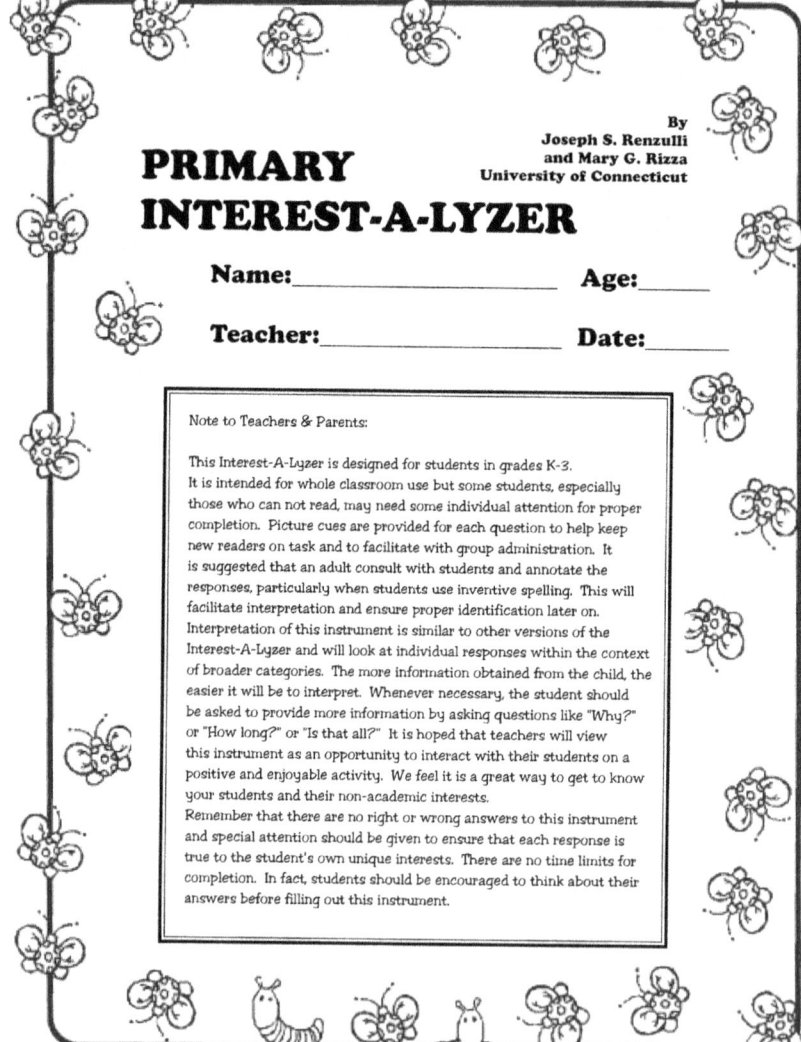

PRIMARY INTEREST-A-LYZER

By
Joseph S. Renzulli
and Mary G. Rizza
University of Connecticut

Name: _____ Age: _____

Teacher: _____ Date: _____

Note to Teachers & Parents:

This Interest-A-Lyzer is designed for students in grades K-3. It is intended for whole classroom use but some students, especially those who can not read, may need some individual attention for proper completion. Picture cues are provided for each question to help keep new readers on task and to facilitate with group administration. It is suggested that an adult consult with students and annotate the responses, particularly when students use inventive spelling. This will facilitate interpretation and ensure proper identification later on. Interpretation of this instrument is similar to other versions of the Interest-A-Lyzer and will look at individual responses within the context of broader categories. The more information obtained from the child, the easier it will be to interpret. Whenever necessary, the student should be asked to provide more information by asking questions like "Why?" or "How long?" or "Is that all?" It is hoped that teachers will view this instrument as an opportunity to interact with their students on a positive and enjoyable activity. We feel it is a great way to get to know your students and their non-academic interests.

Remember that there are no right or wrong answers to this instrument and special attention should be given to ensure that each response is true to the student's own unique interests. There are no time limits for completion. In fact, students should be encouraged to think about their answers before filling out this instrument.

What kinds of books do you like to read?
_____
_____
_____

What is your favorite book?
_____
_____

Do you belong to any clubs or teams?

Tell about them here:
_____
_____
_____
_____

Imagine that you can travel to any time in history.

Where would you go?
_____
_____
_____
_____

You are a famous author about to write your next book, what will it be about?
_____
_____

Can you think of a title?
_____

Name your three favorite T.V. shows here:
_____
_____
_____

Do you have any pets? Tell about them here:
_____
_____

If you could have any pet you wanted, what would it be?
_____
_____

Lots of people play games. What are some of your favorite games?

_____

_____

Have you ever made up a new game? Tell about it here:

_____

_____

_____

Pretend your class is going on a trip and you are in charge of picking the place to go.

Check off 3 ideas from below:

_____ Museum	_____ Science Center
_____ Sports Game	_____ A Show like Ice Capades
_____ Music Concert	_____ Mayor's Office
_____ Newspaper Office	_____ Firehouse
_____ T.V. Studio	_____ Planetarium
_____ Court Room	_____ Police Station
_____ The Zoo	_____ An Amusement Park
_____ A Play	

What did we forget? _____

Pretend you are going to move to the moon with your family and friends. What things will you take with you?

_____
_____
_____
_____

Do you like to collect things? _____

What are some things that you collect?

_____
_____
_____
_____

Some people keep journals where they write stories or poems. Do you have a journal?

_____

What are some things you like to write about?

_____
_____
_____

Some people like to do craft projects. They weave pot holders, string beads, or build things with wood. Do you like to do these kinds of projects?

_____

What are some of the things you make?

_____
_____
_____

Some people like to listen to music.
What is your favorite kind of music?
_____
_____

Do you have a favorite singer or band?
_____
_____

Do you play a musical instrument?
Tell about it here:
_____
_____
_____

Here are things that some people like to do.
Do you like any of them?
Put a check mark next to the ones you like to do.
Circle the ones you would like to try.

____ go to the opera, ballet, play

____ make a secret code

____ help animals

____ speak another language real or imagined

____ make cartoons

____ do science experiments at home

____ plant a garden

____ play a musical instrument

____ sculpt with clay

____ play chess

____ build with legos or other blocks

____ take things apart to see how they work

____ count things (like leaves on a tree or tiles in the floor)

____ cook or bake

____ do jigsaw puzzles

____ play math games

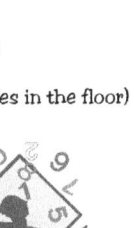

Do you like to draw?
What do you like to draw?
_____
_____

Here is a blank space to draw a picture.

WAIT! WHAT DID WE FORGET?

DO YOU HAVE A SPECIAL INTEREST THAT WE DIDN'T ASK ABOUT?

_____
_____
_____

Appendix F
Action Information Message

ACTION INFORMATION MESSAGE

General Curriculum Area

Activity or Topic

In the space below, provide a brief description of the incident or situation in which you observed high levels of interest, task commitment, or creativity on the part of a student or small group of students. Indicate any areas you may have for advanced-level follow-up activities, suggested resources, or ways to focus the interest into a firsthand investigative experience.

_____
_____
_____
_____
_____
_____
_____
_____
_____
_____

To: _____
From: _____
Date: _____

☐ PLEASE CONTACT ME
☐ I WILL CONTACT YOU TO ARRANGE A MEETING

Date Received: _____   Date of Interview With Child: _____
Date When Services Were Implemented: _____

Appendix G
Management Plan for Individual and Small Group Investigations

Management Plan for Individual and Small-Group Investigations

Name: _____ Grade: _____ Estimated Beginning Date: _____ Ending Date: _____
Teacher: _____ School: _____ Progress Reports Due on Following Dates: _____

General Area(s) of Study (Check all that apply)
- ❑ Language Arts/Humanities
- ❑ Social Studies
- ❑ Mathematics
- ❑ Science
- ❑ Music
- ❑ Art
- ❑ Personal and Social Development
- ❑ Other (Specify) _____
- ❑ Other (Specify) _____

Specify Area of Study
Write a brief description of the problem that you plan to investigate. What are the objectives of your investigation? What do you hope to find out?

Intended Audiences
Which individuals or groups would be most interested in the findings? List the organized groups (clubs, societies, teams) at the local, regional, state, and national levels. What are the names and addresses of contact persons in these groups? When and where do they meet?

1. _____
2. _____
3. _____
4. _____
5. _____

Intended Product(s) and Outlets
What form(s) will the final product take? How, when, and where will you communicate the results of your investigation to an appropriate audience(s)? What outlet vehicles (journals, conferences, art shows, etc.) are typically used by professionals in this field?

Methodological Resources and Activities
List the names and addresses of persons who might provide assistance in attacking this problem. List the how-to books that are available in this area of study. List other resources (films, collections, exhibits, etc.) and special equipment (e.g., camera, tape recorder, questionnaire, etc.). Keep continuous record of all activities that are part of this investigation.

Getting Started
What are the first steps you should take to begin this investigation? What types of information or data will be needed to solve the problem? If "raw data," how can it be gathered, classified, and presented? If you plan to use already categorized information or data, where is it located and how can you obtain what you need?

Appendices ◆ 219

Appendix H
College Services Quiz Answers

1. False
2. False
3. False
4. False
5. True
6. True
7. True
8. False
9. False
10. False

For Product Safety Concerns and Information please contact our EU
representative GPSR@taylorandfrancis.com
Taylor & Francis Verlag GmbH, Kaufingerstraße 24, 80331 München, Germany

www.ingramcontent.com/pod-product-compliance
Lightning Source LLC
Chambersburg PA
CBHW062217300426
44115CB00012BA/2110